FIND
YOUR
FOCUS

5 Steps to
Your Best Year Ever

Endorsements

Success isn't only about setting goals, it's about keeping on track. In **Find Your Focus**, Sarah Arnot Mulhern combines inspiring stories with useful tools to keep you productive and above all, to stay focused on your most important priorities.

Pieter Engelbrecht, CEO, Shoprite Holdings Ltd

We are always looking for ways to make our lives better. In **Find Your Focus** Sarah Arnot Mulhern does a fantastic job encapsulating in very concise and readable terms what we can do to improve our lives and achieve our goals. All of us can take something from this.

His Excellency Liam MacGabhann, Ambassador of Ireland, Embassy of Ireland, Pretoria

Find Your Focus will resonate with anyone asking: "What next?" The book guides you into setting your compass and understanding how to reach your ambitions, whether you are young and setting out on your career journey, or a successful manager who wants to take the next step into corporate leadership.

Deborah Williams, Organisational Development Consultant, MMI

Find Your Focus is a delightful guide full of important information for those of us who want to pursue our goals and enjoy life.

Andile Balula, Eventing SA level 3 course builder, Fédération Équestre International 1* & 2* XC Course Designer

Today we live life on steroids: too much work, too much information, too much stress and too many expectations. Most of us end up complying with our circumstances rather than choosing who, where and what we want to be. This easy-reading, personalised book cuts through the noise and offers five easy steps to a new and better you. There is nothing to lose, so don't wait.

Andrew Woodburn, Managing Director,
Amrop Woodburn Mann Executive Search Africa

Working with Sarah Arnot Mulhern as my coach took away the fear of going into unknown territory. Once the fear was gone, she gave me tools and practical steps to take, and each success gave me the motivation to take the next step. She helped me believe in myself, which gave me confidence in my business and rippled into my personal life as well. What's even more exciting is that now that I have achieved my dream, I'm going to apply the same lessons to aim for even bigger things. **Find Your Focus** shares many of Sarah Arnot Mulhern's stories and the process we used in our work together. My successful and growing business is the proof that it works!

Colette de Vries, Founder, Pilates for Life

Sarah Arnot Mulhern has written a practical guide on how to achieve our dreams. **Find Your Focus** includes a practical and useful guide to achieve our objectives and ultimately transform our lives!

Victor Kotze, CEO, Prosperis

In **Find Your Focus**, Sarah Arnot Mulhern shares stories from the many facets of her life – coaching, the corporate world and sport – to illustrate some of the most recent scientific findings on decisions and choice, how we end up where we are, and what we can do about it. Full of practical suggestions, at the core of the book is a useful process to kickstart thinking about what you want and getting it too. Whether you are starting out in your corporate career, or are at your zenith and thinking, "What next?", this is a great book to read from cover to cover and then to keep on hand to dip into as you need it.

Francois Strydom, Executive, EOH Legal Services

I have witnessed first-hand Sarah Arnot Mulhern's ability to influence, change, motivate and lead a diverse group of people from good to great. As an athlete, she embodies the word 'grit', which can be described as a great blend of passion and perseverance. Her book is not a dry academic body of work. She has skilfully made it an inspiring piece of literature – kept alive by the stories woven appropriately into the themes. This book is a must-read for anyone with a dream!

Phil Cunningham, Founder, Sunrise Productions

Find Your Focus contains many real-life adventures from Sarah Arnot Mulhern's own coaching experience. To be given exposure to other CEOs' thinking via her coaching model and their fuel for success is enriching. This is a book I will be sharing with my leadership team.

Derek Patrick, CEO, The Design Company

As an academic coach, I find Sarah Arnot Mulhern's practical five steps to be an essential ingredient towards the ultimate success of each client's graduation – reaching their own 'further shore'. I highly recommend this book to anyone who is on a journey of personal, professional, or vocational development. Sarah Arnot Mulhern's powerful stories are truly inspiring and I intend to share her book with all those who cross my path.

Caroline Dale, Director, The Thesis Coach

First published in 2019.

ISBN: 978-1-86922-804-0
eISBN: 978-1-86922-805-7 (ePDF)

Published by KR Publishing
P O Box 3954
Randburg
2125
Republic of South Africa

Tel: (011) 706-6009
Fax: (011) 706-1127
E-mail: orders@knowres.co.za
Website: www.kr.co.za

 Typesetting, layout and design: Cia Joubert, cia@knowres.co.za
Cover design: Marlene de'Lorme, marlene@knowres.co.za
Editing & proofreading: Jennifer Renton, jenniferrenton@live.co.za
Project management: Cia Joubert, cia@knowres.co.za

FIND YOUR FOCUS

5 Steps to
Your Best Year Ever

by

Sarah Arnot Mulhern

kr
publishing

2019

From the chorus of
The Cure at Troy

Human beings suffer,
They torture one another,
They get hurt and get hard.
No poem or play or song
Can fully right a wrong
Inflicted and endured.

The innocent in gaols
Beat on their bars together.
A hunger-striker's father
Stands in the graveyard dumb.
The police widow in veils
Faints at the funeral home.

History says, don't hope
On this side of the grave.
But then, once in a lifetime
The longed-for tidal wave
Of justice can rise up,
And hope and history rhyme.

So hope for a great sea-change
On the far side of revenge.
Believe that further shore
Is reachable from here.
Believe in miracles
And cures and healing wells.

Call miracle self-healing:
The utter, self-revealing
Double-take of feeling.
If there's fire on the mountain
Or lightning and storm
And a god speaks from the sky

That means someone is hearing
The outcry and the birth-cry
Of new life at its term.

Seamus Heaney

Table of Contents

Table of Figures

Acknowledgements

This approach to setting objectives has been around for a while. I've seen a version of it from James Clear, who has a blog well worth following: http://www.jamesclear.com.

I've seen and used another version from Kate Harrison, author of *The 5:2 diet*, which I've been following for years: http://kate-harrison.com/5-2diet.

Thank you to both of them for the inspiration to write this book.

I would like to express deep gratitude to my coaching clients, especially to those who have allowed me to share their stories in this book. Thank you also to my colleagues at the Woodburn Mann Leadership Science Institute and to my ex-colleagues at Spencer Stuart. Special recognition goes to the Western Cape Eventing Association council members – we had a lot of fun and a glorious nine years together. I've been lucky for the past two years to be Chairman of the Stellenbosch and District Riding Club and in that time the team has achieved outcomes beyond what I thought was possible. If I have something to say, it's thanks to all of you.

I'm incredibly lucky to have my brothers, Graham Mulhern and Mark Mulhern, and bless technology for enabling us to stay such close siblings and friends even though we live so far apart. You constantly challenge me to push harder and think further; I could not do it without you.

A book takes a huge amount of effort and input from an array of people. I would particularly like to thank the people who reviewed early or late versions of the text and offered critical feedback and support. Caroline Dale, Victor Kotze and Deborah Williams, you are a remarkable trio of friends and your support and encouragement mean so much. My stepchildren, Robyn, Lauren, Christopher and Alistair (step-in-law), helped me edit the first edition of this book and gave me great comments and insights. How lucky I am that you have become my family.

Thank you to Ilze Visage who created the beautiful illustrations in this book.

I first laid eyes on Sophie Kevany more than 40 years ago when I started at Rathdown School; we were just nine years old. Our friendship has endured time and change and is precious beyond words. Sophie is a professional writer and journalist and helped edit this book. Any mistakes are mine, and were it not for Sophie's eagle eye, there would be many more.

About the author

Sarah Arnot Mulhern is Managing Partner of the Woodburn Mann Leadership Science Institute, which provides leadership development and assessment services to Boards, CEOs and senior executives in Southern African corporate businesses. The Woodburn Mann Leadership Science Institute brings the science of leadership to the boardrooms of Africa.

Sarah's career spans more than 25 years, most of it spent at two companies – Accenture and Spencer Stuart – based in Ireland, France, the UK and South Africa. She held international leadership roles in both organisations. As an executive search consultant at Spencer Stuart she led the European Internet Practice and the European Software Practice. After moving to South Africa, she joined the Leadership Advisory Services (LAS) practice, consulting to global clients in multiple industries.

Sarah gives motivational talks based on her experience in sport and business and offers expert leadership advice on television and radio.

Sarah is also an amateur three-day eventer, which is a three-phase Olympic equestrian sport that includes dressage, show jumping and cross country. She has held leadership roles in the sport, acting as President of Western Cape Eventing for nine years and sitting on the Board of Eventing SA.

Sarah holds BA (Hons) and MA degrees from Trinity College, Dublin and an MPhil (Executive Coaching) from the University of Stellenbosch Business School.

Preface

For almost 20 years my job has been to interview and assess senior executives all over the world. The interviews happened for one of two reasons: either I was headhunting them (headhunting is the informal term we use for finding high level executive staff), or I was helping a company identify and develop executives for a big role, like CEO, a process known as succession planning. During those years, I began to realise that most executives fell into two broad categories, neither of which had anything to do with culture, education or training. They either took control of their career path, or they let their career happen to them. Turning my attention to my friends and acquaintances I saw the same thing happening. No matter who they are, people often allow life to happen to them, responding to opportunities instead of deciding what they want out of life. I probably fell into the more passive category until I came across a unique approach to choosing what you want and working out how to get it. There's nothing wrong with taking advantage of opportunities when they come up, but why wait? Why not create your own?

As I began to understand more about pro-active life planning, I decided to gather my experiences, and those of my clients, into a book and combine it with academic research on leadership and human behaviour. This is that book. It is full of stories, research, ideas and inspiration, and it offers a 5-Step process to help you apply that science to your life, changing it forever and for the better.

I understand that life can be hard. I've had my fair share of sadness, maybe more than my fair share, so I speak from experience. Hope keeps me going when the tough times come. The hope that with time, and if we make the right choices, things will change. That is the theme of the chorus of Seamus Heaney's *The Cure at Troy*.

Your life.
How to discover what you want,
then make sure you get it.

Introduction

D o you know what you want out of life? Or even out of one year of your life: this year?

This book helps you to identify what you really want to focus on, and then to put a plan in place to deliver exactly that. How simple does that sound? It's quite a straightforward concept and, if you are keen to get going and make your plan for the year, then head along to Part Three and get started. You can come back to some of the stories and insights when you are done. But just before you go... a bit of context to this second edition.

We published the first edition of this book, *That Further Shore*, in June 2018. Since then, I have collected feedback from clients and friends on how useful they found the 5-Step process. The response was unexpected. Every single person who followed the plan and wrote down their themes and objectives achieved almost all of them. Even if they did not look at the plan again in the months that followed, when they went back to read it at the end of the year, they found they had achieved their objectives. And even found them easy to achieve.

Many others told me that they found it too hard to pin down their themes and objectives, so they gave up before they had finished the five steps. Because they did not set objectives, it was hard to tell what they had achieved.

I cannot promise you that if you write down what you want, on paper, as described in this book, you will get it. No-one can promise you that. But there's strong evidence that if you do put some objectives down on paper and think about how you are going to achieve them, you'll do just that.

I picked three themes for myself in 2017. Work, study and eventing. Eventing is an equestrian Olympic sport that involves three disciplines: dressage, cross country and show jumping. Training for all three is time-consuming.

One of my objectives was to qualify for the next level and I did not achieve it until 2018. I feel quite good about it though, because I had clear priorities: first study, then work, then sport. I sacrificed quite a few competitions to put in enough study hours to complete my MPhil. Then my horse hurt himself, not seriously, but enough to miss the 2017 South African Championships. I ride for fun and that means I cannot always prioritise it the way I would like to. In the meantime, though, I nailed my other objectives. In fact, I wish I'd set even bigger ones. More about that later.

Before you head off to the 5-Step process in Part Three, I would like to tell you about some of the challenges my clients have faced. There's a lot of research available on human behaviour and why we behave the way we do, but research is dry and can be dull to read. Stories are more interesting and I have chosen some of the best. They illustrate how certain behaviours can help or hinder us. In all of them, goals are a key theme. When we challenge ourselves with goals, we have to figure out how we are going to change our behaviour in order to achieve those goals. These stories are mostly about those changes.

I cannot thank my clients enough for allowing me to talk about our work together. Some names have been changed and some are real. Sometimes the stories come from several clients and have been combined for simplicity.

As well as writing out goals, one of the key elements of coaching is conversations that help you understand what you want. You could see this book as a coaching conversation, full of real life examples that show how people's lives can change when they take control.

No matter how good coaching is, it cannot change your life. Only you can do that. A good coach is no more than a sounding board and a catalyst, helping people to explore their thinking and make better choices. Choices that already exist, but only become obvious when we take the time to think more deeply.

Some of the stories are specifically about leadership. Leadership theory applies to us all, because each of us is our own leader. That means anything you read about leadership applies directly to you and your goals. That is one of the main themes of this book: be your own leader, and above all, be true and honest with yourself.

The next theme is about setting some big goals. In the past I've recommended setting achievable goals, but my ongoing study of business and sports changed my view. If the friends and clients who followed the 5-Step process last year achieved their objectives with ease, maybe they could have set bigger goals?

Of course there are times when it's sensible to set SMART (Specific, Measurable, Achievable, Realistic and Timed) goals, but there are other times when you want to be ambitious; to see if you can achieve the unthinkable. This year I'm going big and, if it's the right time for you, I encourage you to go big too.

If this is your year: Go Big.

When you set your goal at 100, you achieve 100. When you set it at 1000 you might only achieve 500, but that is still five times more than 100.

The third theme might be the most important.

If you want to achieve greater success you are going to have to do things a bit differently, and that requires learning.

I've accrued many benefits from years spent studying coaching and working with leaders. One of those is a far better understanding of adult learning. As adults, we learn differently from children. Some people like to think and model things in their own mind before they'll try something new. Others like to jump right in and learn as they go. It doesn't matter which type of learner you are, the important thing is: never stop learning.

The challenge is that learning requires humility.

In sport, people run up against this problem all the time. They might learn to ride a horse, maybe even get a good horse and win a few prizes. Then a really good trainer comes into town. All too often, instead of taking every word this trainer says as a pearl of wisdom and applying it to what they do, the rider goes into the lesson thinking, "I'll show them how good I am". They seek praise, not constructive criticism. And some might even resent the constructive criticism offered. Yet no matter how good you think you are, there will be constructive criticism you can take on board if you are ready. As an adult it can be hard to be the student again, but adjusting your mindset to become a seeker of information and knowledge is the only path to growth and change. All that's needed is a degree of humility.

I've spent a lot of time thinking about humility because I've realised it takes some confidence to be humble, and sometimes I lack confidence. I know I'm not the only one who struggles with this. To be humble you have to accept that others are better than you; that they know more than you do. That's not always easy, but it's definitely worth thinking about. With humility comes the appreciation that we can learn from others; indeed that we can learn something from everyone. Open your mind to learning, from books and online sources, as well as from all those around you.

In Part One of this book, you'll find stories and themes from my life and from some of my coaching clients. In Part Two, there are tools and techniques that help keep us all on track as we set out to achieve our dreams. In Part Three, you'll find the 5-Step process that will set you on the road to achieving those dreams.

At the back of the book I've included an appendix that gives you the 5-Step process without the additional stories and information. When you come back to do your plan again, maybe at the end of the year, you might find it helpful to go straight to that appendix to remind yourself of the process and key ideas.

> This is your book. If you follow the 5-Step process, you will reach that further shore and achieve your dreams. Please let me know how it goes.

- saraharnotconsulting@gmail.com;
- www.woodburnmannlsi.co.za;
- linkedin.com/in/sarah-arnot-39546a
- sarah.arnot@wmlsi.co.za

Part One – Believe that further shore is reachable from here

"If it doesn't challenge you, it won't change you."

Competeeveryday.com

Chapter 1

The story of an entrepreneur

❧

I met Colette after I'd broken my back falling off a horse. For my whole life I had imagined that this would be the worst thing that could happen to me, so when I hit the ground hard one day at the Riding Club in Noordhoek, a suburb of Cape Town, I immediately knew something was wrong. I stayed absolutely still and remember thinking: "This is a really bad fall". My second thought was, "Wow, this is a really good hat". That was because, as I flew through the air like a torpedo, I proved to my full satisfaction that the head is indeed the heaviest part of the body, ensuring I smashed into the ground skull-first.

The paramedics delicately loaded me onto a backboard that immobilised my spine and carted me off by ambulance to Constantiaberg Hospital. I will never forget the ER doctor, who had just looked at the x-rays, telling me I was fine. She said, "You have to learn to differentiate between muscle pain, rather than bone pain", as she pushed her finger hard into my C7 vertebra, later found to be broken in two places. "I'm pretty sure that's bone pain", I said, wincing. "No, you're fine, you can go home", she said dismissively, evidently thinking I was making a fuss about nothing.

By then I'd been immobilised on a back board for about four hours with, as we later discovered, seven fractures in my vertebrae. To add to the damage, at precisely the point where the nerves run out of the spinal cord, the whole area was now stiff and inflamed. Sitting up from that back board was the most painful thing I've ever done. It hurts even to think about it.

I spent most of the following week lying on a pile of pillows, working on an urgent client project. I had to cancel a trip to Johannesburg to assess a senior executive, but they insisted I saw him anyway, even if they had to bring him to me, because I was the only person available with the necessary expertise. I could barely move, and certainly couldn't drive, but clients come first, as they always do. My employer organised a driver to collect me from home and take me to a hotel in Stellenbosch where I did the four-hour long assessment, a pillow at my back. The colleague who sat in the interview told me afterwards: "I couldn't even look at you; the pain was written across your face." Happily, the candidate, who was up for the job of Chief HR Officer at a major company, later told me he noticed nothing wrong. To my surprise, there wasn't too much wrong with the report I wrote either. That meant that somehow, I had managed to focus on the assessment and deliver the result.

For the rest of that week, if I did nothing more than move my fingers across the keyboard, I was ok. But the second I did anything more active, I marvelled at the pain. On the sixth night, I was getting tingling down my arms and I thought, "This isn't right".

The next morning I went to my local doctor. She said I was probably fine, but loaded me up with serious painkillers and sent me to Dr Jack Eksteen, a spinal surgeon, to make sure.

Dr Eksteen immediately sent me for an MRI. When they saw the soft tissue damage on the image, the radiologists popped me straight into the CT scanner. That scan finally revealed seven broken bones, including two on the very C7 the ER doctor had jabbed when she said I was fine. It wasn't really her fault. These little fractures are hard to identify without a CT scan because a normal x-ray machine cannot get the right angle. Luckily it was the spinal processes that had snapped – those little wings that stick out of each vertebra. That meant my spinal cord was not compromised and the fractures were stable. It was just as well that I had not tripped and fallen during that first week, though, and it certainly explained the pain.

South Africa is a sports mad country and a lot of people, including doctors, compete in extreme sports. Races like the 80KM Comrades Marathon, the eight-day Cape Epic Mountain Bike Race (624KM), or the four day Berg River Canoe Marathon (240KM) are considered quite normal. An everyday 42KM marathon is seen as a 5KM Park Run to sports enthusiasts here. Whereas in Europe doctors preach caution, here, many of them enjoy participating in extreme or dangerous sports just like everyone else. For this reason they understand that while you may be seriously injured, it doesn't quench your desire to participate.

Dr Eksteen is a particularly keen motor bike rider, surely ironic for a spinal surgeon in a country with one of the highest road accident death rates in the world. He completely understood that my main objective was to get back on a horse. Because my fractures were stable, he chose not to operate and fuse the spine, assuring me that if I put up with the pain and was patient, letting the bones heal on their own, I would have much better movement once I recovered. "You're tough and stoic enough, Sarah", he said, "you'll be fine". I didn't feel particularly tough or stoic, but I didn't want spinal surgery either so I agreed to his plan.

Nine months later the bones finally healed and he gave me the green light to get back on a horse, though he did make me promise to wear an air jacket when jumping. The air jacket was originally invented for motor bike riders; it's a light waistcoat that attaches to your saddle, so if you fall, it inflates before you hit the ground. Had I been wearing one when I fell that day at Noordhoek, the hyperextension that snapped all those little bones could not have happened. I have worn one ever since.

Dr Eksteen also told me I would need to do Pilates for the rest of my life to help manage the ongoing consequences of such a major spinal trauma. When nerves are badly damaged the muscles spasm, but Pilates and associated exercises can help lengthen and strengthen the muscles, reducing the spasms and the consequent pain.

He suggested that I contact Colette De Vries who runs Pilates For Life in my hometown of Paarl, telling me she would know exactly how to handle my injuries and get me back to competitive riding. He was so right. Colette not only got me back to competition level, but she helped transform my rather unwilling and unathletic body, turning me into a far better, stronger rider. As soon as I started working with Colette, I realised she was world class and that I was incredibly lucky to have found her. She enabled me to counteract my muscular-skeletal damage, caused not only by the fall, but by 25 years on planes, behind desks and working on laptops, allowing me to develop a fit, more flexible and capable body that moves with, not against, the horse. The proof is in my "before Colette" and "after Colette" videos. She has also become one of my closest friends.

Colette combines many of the attributes necessary for business success. Firstly, she is 100% committed to lifelong learning. Although she qualified long ago and trains both clients and instructors, she spends weekends studying exercise and movement, and regularly attends courses to increase and refresh her knowledge. She has a small business and a limited budget, and until recently, held classes at home in Paarl in a converted garage.

Colette has a warm personality and a great sense of humour, which means classes with her are fun, as well as demanding and highly engaging. Having watched her teach students who are aspiring Pilates instructors, I've seen first-hand how she places the wellbeing of her clients first. She tells her students that how they are feeling on any given day is of no importance to the people they teach. Their job is to turn up on time, indeed five minutes early, with a smile on their face and a heart open to the client's needs. As teachers, their focus must be outwards, not inwards.

So many of us working in business could benefit from this advice and over the years I've seen Colette put it into practice every day, no matter how she is feeling.

In 2016, Colette could not sleep at night. She is a devoted mother with three children. Her middle son, Dante, is an exceptional rugby player and was on the legendary First team at his school, Paarl Boys High. In his final year, he was offered the chance to attend university in the UK and play rugby for the local team. Of course he wanted to do it, and Colette felt she could not hold her son back.

The problem was that three years of UK university fees is a lot of Pilates classes, particularly when those classes are in a weak and unstable currency like the South African Rand. She was also worried that her dream of building a really great Pilates studio was slipping away. In short, her goal was to find a beautiful space where she could grow her business, but fear was holding her back.

By 2016 I was working on my MPhil in Executive Coaching at the University of Stellenbosch Business School. Part of the requirement was that I experiment with different coaching techniques, working with real coaching clients. I had a number of fairly senior corporate clients and this kind of experimentation would not have been appropriate for them. They were paying me for my time and their needs came first, not mine.

Meanwhile, I realised my friend Colette had a business challenge, one I thought I could help her with. I also thought we might have some fun playing with these different techniques. Dedicated as she is to learning, Colette could not have been happier to help and potentially reap some rewards for her own life and business. Generally, I don't like to coach my friends, but in this situation I felt both of us understood and could manage the boundaries.

Storytelling is at the heart of coaching. Equally important is listening. Basically, to get somewhere, clients need to tell their story to someone who is really listening. In doing that, they must first make sense of it.

As Colette told me her story it was obvious to both of us that there were plenty of actions she could take that would start a process of change in her business.

We used some tools to help her generate ideas, including a simple SWOT (strengths, weaknesses, opportunities and threats) analysis, which helped identify some ideas for solving problems.

Strengths

o   Solid client base
o   Beginning of a good team in place
o   Ability to bring in and train more staff
o   Trusted by medical profession – a source of new clients
o   Hardworking and ambitious
o   Great personality for this kind of work
o   Excellent technical skills
o   Willing to continue investing and training
o   Amazing existing clients, which is why I love doing this

Weaknesses

o   Spending too much time on admin tasks
o   Not marketing the business enough
o   Too dependent on me as the trainer, need to develop the profile and client base of the other trainers
o   Working from own home – means the family sometimes feel invaded
o   No funds to finance expansion
o   Hard to find the right location
o   Feeling under financial pressure which could limit ability to act and grow

Opportunities

o   Influx of higher-earning clients to the local area – estates such as Val de Vie and Pearl Valley as well as Paarl itself
o   Development in the town may lead to a suitable location
o   Could expand the team and teach them how to bring in new clients as well as training them to teach Pilates
o   More studios can generate more income
o   Don't wait to find the perfect place, start growing the business and finding the right people now

Threats

o   Ex-students setting up competing studios (not a serious threat)
o   Inability to invest enough in the new studio
o   Haven't found the right property
o   Expanding feels risky, fear is paralysing
o   Not setting sights high enough
o   Finding the time to look for premises and set up new studios as well as teaching to bring income in
o   Find the right people for the long term team
o   Not spending enough time marketing; people seem to think we are "full"

Figure 1: Pilates for Life SWOT analysis

The next step was for Colette to begin thinking about her business in a structured way. Together we created buckets that included HR, admin, sales and marketing, property, etc., and sorted the output of the SWOT analysis and other ideas into those buckets.

PILATES FOR LIFE

HR

Develop the team
Find more people
Face up to the
people issues (be
more demanding,
this is really hard)
Think about who to
hire as I grow the
business

SALES & MARKETING

People keep saying "oh I
hear you are full"; change
that perception
Spend more time marketing
the business
Find new marketing
strategies
This section is the most
important, need to work on
it all the time
Get help? How?

TRAINING

Training is a source of
potential new income
Hard work – means
no weekend off,
something I love
doing to have time
for research for the
courses and myself

ADMIN

Stop spending time on
admin someone else
could do
Find an admin
assistant – part time
to start?
Finance – need to
raise funds when I
decide on property,
where and how?

PROPERTY

This is the other big one,
finding a property where
I can develop the "dream
studio" is really hard. Keep
looking for properties
Put together a list of
must haves, nice to haves
and don't wants to make
it easier and quicker to
investigate opportunities

CLIENTS

Clients need to know how
important they are to me,
their wellbeing is why I
do this (purpose, mission
statement?)
Clients also a source of
new clients
Always try and exceed
clients' expectations
World class Pilates

Figure 2: Pilates for Life buckets

It did not matter at that stage if there was only one person in the HR bucket and zero in the admin one. The idea was to put some shape and structure around the business. Actions quickly emerged from that exercise, enabling Colette to think in a more systemic and structured way about how to move forward. For example, she did not have any administrative assistance, so she was spending time on tasks that were not helping to grow the business in any way. She quickly found someone to help with her administration in return for Pilates training.

Eighteen months later, having grown the business considerably, Colette partnered with the owner of Spice Route wine farm on the outskirts of Paarl, where she finally designed her dream studio. The studio is world class and has attracted many more clients. Her reputation has spread fast and international Pilates experts, who have heard of her well-equipped studio in the Cape Winelands, now fly in to run clinics at Pilates For Life.

Today, with three fully equipped studios and a range of different classes, Colette continues to grow the business. She has also been able to grow her Pilates teacher training practice, already popular because of her unique style and huge knowledge base. Best of all, her son Dante went to university in Leeds and played rugby for the local team. He graduated in 2018 with an excellent degree in business studies and a scholarship to continue with a Master's degree.

The point of the story is not to tell you that coaching helped Colette, although she gives our coaching sessions a lot of credit for where she is today. The point is that the only thing stopping Colette from achieving her dream was fear of taking action. In her case, taking action meant analysing her situation to understand what was important, and then taking the steps that would lead to change and growth. For many people, translating ambition into action is the hardest step. That means the simpler you make the first steps, the easier it is to begin. Not everything Colette identified worked immediately, for example she explored several different venues before finding the right one. Because she had sorted her actions into categories, or buckets, she was able to see that she was making progress in some areas while others took longer. Knowing she was progressing, even if only in one area, helped maintain her confidence and tenacity in the other areas.

That progress motivated her to keep going with the bigger picture in mind.

Inspiration and motivation

❦

*T*he *Power of Small Wins* by Teresa M. Amabile and Steven J. Kramer was published in the *Harvard Business Review*, a publication I often use as a resource for articles on leadership. Not only is their writing based on solid academic research, but they use clear, straightforward business language which makes them easier to read than articles published in academic journals.

When Amabile and Kramer studied motivation, they found, somewhat to their surprise, that although people are motivated by power and money as you might expect, what motivates us most of all is a feeling of progress, or what the authors call "small wins".

That is why it makes sense to first identify your true ambitions, then clarify outcomes and sort them into clear objectives, and finally, to break out the component pieces. All of that makes the likelihood of small wins much greater, breeding confidence, as it did for Colette.

> If you feel you are making progress in some areas, it will help motivate you to keep going in others, where it might be tougher and require more persistence to achieve a breakthrough.

Another article talks about persistence being the main factor that leads to success, particularly for entrepreneurs. Most businesses don't fail because they weren't good ideas – they fail because people gave up too soon. I love the story of James Dyson, who went through hundreds, if not thousands, of iterations before he perfected his eponymous cleaner and changed vacuuming forever. Constant innovation and persistence led him to succeed. Along the way Dyson almost certainly had small wins that helped him to persist.

I recently listened to Arnold Schwarzenegger's autobiography, *Total Recall*. Anyone who knows me might be surprised to find me reading/listening to the action hero, body-builder's autobiography, so here is how it came about. I was reading *Tools of Titans*, a rather hefty book by Tim Ferriss that is packed full of great ideas and wonderful insights. *Tools of Titans* summarises the best content from the many leaders and thinkers Ferriss has interviewed over the years for his podcast. One of the interviews was with Schwarzenegger and I decided to listen because I always wondered how on earth a Mr Universe from Austria came to marry a Kennedy, become a huge movie star and then Governor of California. The interview in *Tools of Titans* surprised me, not least because Schwarzenegger came across as playful, intelligent and very hard working. When I saw he'd written his autobiography my curiosity was piqued, so I listened to the audiobook and loved it. Schwarzenegger is energetic, thoughtful, humorous, open-minded and clear about his ideas. He's also flawed, as all the best people are, and he's quite private, so I'm sure there's a lot that did not make it into the book. He has a great memory and goes into detail about the early part of his career, when a lot of his learning about life took place.

One of the first things in the book to strike me was something he said about body building. He said, "My body really responded". This means he gained small wins all the time, which encouraged him to keep going, persisting over many years with weight-lifting repetitions in his quest to attain a form of physical perfection.

This was a revelation because it explains why I find exercising so profoundly unrewarding. Since my early 20s I've run approximately 4km about three times a week; sometimes more, sometimes less. Occasionally I do a longer run, up to 10km. I will never run further than that; my body simply doesn't respond to all this exercise. For years I pushed harder by doing interval training and I even ended up with Athlete's Heart Syndrome, which was diagnosed when my resting heart rate dropped to the low 40s and became irregular and quite uncomfortable. This is frankly ridiculous when you only run 40 minutes three times a week, even if you are doing interval training. My sports mad, Comrades Marathon running doctor thought it was very funny and admitted he was a bit jealous. He couldn't get his own heartrate below 55. I did not think it was funny at all, and that strange heartbeat didn't go away until I broke my back and couldn't run for several months.

Once I recovered, I was back to running as soon as I could, although I dropped the interval training and I don't push myself to the max anymore. But why, despite the lack of reward, have I been hauling myself out there three times a week for the last 25 years? What is motivating me? What are the small wins that keep me going through the seasons and the years, and, hopefully, many years to come?

I run for many reasons. It doesn't help me to lose weight, but I suspect it may help prevent me gaining it, and I've joked that I run away from the fat person I don't want to be. When I travel, having a pair of running shoes means I can always exercise, in a hotel gym if I have to.

Then there's the fact that I like being outside and enjoy what I see around me. To say nothing of the post-run euphoria, which is terrific. I always try to run first thing in the morning, when my motivation is highest. Cities are more interesting at that time of day, before the general populace is on the move. The farm where I live is beautiful at dawn. So is my hometown, in Ireland's County

Wicklow. But, perhaps most important of all, there's the thinking I do. That free ranging state of mind that Mihaly Csikszentmihalyi calls "flow". Just being out in the air, not thinking about anything in particular and letting the body move freely, liberates my thinking, allowing it to range across any number of topics and come up with new ideas. I appreciate this so much that I don't even listen to music when I run. Where else do you spend 40 minutes with no distractions, no messages, no email, no Facebook, not driving, or talking, or sitting in a meeting? Not thinking about what you need to do, nor rushing through to the next item? There's nothing but putting one foot in front of the other in the morning air. That in itself is a "win". And no matter how hard it is to keep putting one foot in front of the other, I never regret it once I'm out there. I know I can survive the 40 minutes, and that too sustains motivation, keeping me running week in, week out. Year in, year out.

> You don't always have to chase a big goal; sometimes it's the small commitment, like the running, that keeps us in good health over the years, giving us the consistent small wins that sustain motivation over extended periods of time.

Whether your goals are large or small I encourage you to apply the 5-Step process in Part Three to figure out your themes and objectives. Then you can work out how to achieve them by breaking each objective into small, manageable steps to get you started.

The same planning process works with teams: all it takes is a flip chart or a big white board, and a brainstorming session. Only one warning: I've found teams often come up with a plethora of great ideas, but they find it really hard to whittle them down to just three to five themes for the year. They want to do it all. The reality is that if you have too many themes you might not achieve any of them.

That means staying focused on the most important themes; the ones where you most want to move the dial and achieve results.

The other ideas can be a back-up, so if you unexpectedly deliver early, you can add stretch by updating the list.

Chapter 3

Choices and frames

❧

Sometimes you'll accidently restrict yourself because you unconsciously limit your choices. Coaches see this a lot and it's an aspect of behavioural economics that plays into the coaching process, something I'll explain after I've told you about Jerome.

Jerome works for a major insurance firm and was identified early on by his boss as someone who takes ownership, gets the job done and delivers. Whenever his boss changed jobs, he made sure to bring Jerome along with him, which has led to some interesting career development opportunities.

Yet Jerome reached a stage where he felt stuck. He had grown and changed into a more mature and competent leader, but his boss was still seeing the same person he had always seen. This meant that Jerome did not always receive the credit and opportunities he deserved.

Jerome was so frustrated that he was thinking of leaving the business. "Before you do that Jerome", I said, "let's just talk about the situation and whether you have the power to change some of the things you don't like. Rather than move away to another company, which might be no better, why don't we look at identifying what you really want and see if you can get it here and now?"

The company is one with a reputation for treating employees well, particularly in terms of training and career development, so I genuinely felt that Jerome should explore all his options before taking a decision that might not benefit him in the long term.

We talked about the challenge and I asked him, "Who is responsible for your career development?" "My boss", was the reply. "Really?" I asked. "Yes, but nothing is happening." So I asked, "What can you do about that?" Jerome paused and thought for a long moment. "I suppose I could take the responsibility myself?" My next question was, "If you did, if you had the freedom to do that, what kind of choices would you make?" Enthusiasm began to sound in Jerome's voice. "I could make a plan of what I wanted, and then start working towards that." "Would it change your relationship with your boss?" I asked. Another long pause. "You know, I think it would", said Jerome. "I wouldn't feel I depended on him so much. In fact, it might make me feel like I owned the relationship and I could start managing the relationship and taking responsibility for it." His face lit up as he thought about it.

Our next session was about a month later and the man who walked into our meeting room was a completely different person. His face was alive and before I could say a word he said:

"Sarah, I have to tell you, this has been the most amazing month of my life. After our meeting, I suddenly realized that I own my job, and what I do, and that I can change the relationships around me if I want to. I went to my boss with a plan. I didn't ask his permission, I just calmly told him what I was going to do, with the team, and for my own development. When he didn't give it his full attention, I called him on that and told him that he needed to take his management role more seriously. At first, he was surprised, but then he responded really well. He started looking at me differently and from then on, he saw me differently. Even in meetings he's been treating me with respect and he steps back when I speak up. I cannot believe how easy it was to change things and how much better I feel. I've been looking forward to this session so much so that I can tell you all about it."

Jerome continued in this vein for the rest of our session. From that moment on our coaching sessions were about using me as a sounding board for his ideas. Any thoughts of his leaving the business evaporated.

Jerome had found himself in a position where he did not believe he had the power to change things. He was frustrated and unhappy and thought his only choice lay in the status quo or leaving the company.

That kind of overly narrow framing of situations is a key topic in Daniel Kahneman's brilliant book, *Thinking Fast and Slow*. He shows how easily we fall into the trap of thinking that our choices are binary; that we have to choose between two options. If we broaden our frames and look at things differently, many more choices start to emerge.

Having a coach who listens with undivided attention and asks good questions can help clients broaden their frames. The questions I asked Jerome were not particularly earth-shattering or sophisticated, but they helped him to think differently about his situation. Note the wording there... the coaching did not change Jerome's world, it was merely the catalyst that helped him change his own world.

Simple as it may seem, the personal brainstorming in the 5-Step process can help you broaden your frame and move beyond binary choices.

I love to bounce ideas off others, but sometimes that's not possible. When it's not, I apply Step 3 of the 5-Step process. I make myself sit down with a sheet of paper and spend five or ten minutes writing down everything I can think of about the question at hand, with a focus on positive outcomes. It's like a mini, self-driven coaching session. I'm not particularly creative but I'm often amazed at what my mind comes up with when I force it to concentrate hard on something specific for a short period of time.

As you come up with more options and a greater range of choices using the 5-Step process, you may end up setting objectives or prioritising unexpected themes. There's nothing wrong with that. On the contrary, if that happens you should be proud of your work; it means you've identified new choices and potential for a greater range of possibilities.

In this chapter I've focused on encouraging you to use the brainstorming process in Step 3 to broaden your frame of choices. There's another important aspect to choice: are the decisions we make every day bringing us closer to our goals or pushing us further away? We're going to take a closer look at that when we get to Part Two.

Chapter 4

Process

❦

Having a plan is a big part of achieving your goals. This book will help you figure out the actions you need to take for your plan to become reality. That is what we call "process" – and anything you want to do well will involve a process of some kind.

The trouble is that perfecting a process is often boring, or just plain hard work. In sport, it's the hours and hours of practice you put in; the training and the fine tuning and the constant challenging of your limits. In business, it's constantly improving your skills. As a leader that might mean intense periods of training, extra reading about management and leadership, improving your financial skills, or constant operational improvements.

For example, if you have never done it before, you might want to invest in presentation skills – not only how to stand up and present, but also how to create great presentations and deliver powerful messages. There's so much available through the internet that can help you improve your processes, yet because it's the boring bit, we don't always do that. But remember, when the chips are down, the person or the business with the best processes wins. You want to be that person.

There's a great piece about this in James Kerr's *Legacy*, which is the story of how the All Blacks transformed a weak team in the mid-2000s into the winning machine they are now. The All Blacks' team management decided that they would examine every single process involved in delivering a world-beating game of rugby on the field and look for ways to improve each one. They figured that it might be very hard to improve a single process by 10%, but if you could identify a 1% improvement across many processes, you might end up with 10% improvement, or even much more.

Schwarzenegger talks about process in *Total Recall* and I like what he has to say. What is relevant is his commitment to repetitions: what he calls reps. He learned early on, when he started building that famous body, that it's the commitment to reps that gets the result – which, back then, was winning Mr Universe. He would make a plan for a long training session, decide what he wanted to do and chalk up lines on the wall of the gym in the small town where he lived in Austria. When he finished each series of reps he would put a cross through the line, until all the lines, maybe 50 or 60 in a session, were crossed off.

Later, as Governor of California, a state far bigger than many small countries, he would still be there with his list of commitments, crossing them off one by one. As an action hero in films he does his own stunts because they can never find a body double who looks like him. To learn the hard stunts, he would do the reps. Say a scene required him to ride a motor bike backwards, shooting at his opponent. He would practice handling the gun, then riding the bike, then turning around and riding the bike backwards, then riding the bike backwards handling the gun. On and on until it was just right, so that when the cameras rolled the stunt was a single, perfect take.

Breaking something down into its component parts and then building it up again until you've got it right is central to achieving your goals. This doesn't just apply to sport. For example, self-management is an important part of leadership. Applying process to self-management involves researching it, understanding the component parts and then "doing the reps". In the case of self-management that might mean responding calmly and consistently even when other people get heated. Or committing only to those things you really will deliver. In that case, doing the reps is about delivering every time, so that it becomes a smooth consistent routine that your colleagues can rely on.

On its own, process is not enough; you need to improve and refine all the time. Schwarzenegger became particularly adept at looking at his own body from a neutral perspective, identifying weaknesses and then adjusting his training programme to address them. Most of us need to identify the process and then push ourselves out of our comfort zone, where we might make mistakes or even scare ourselves. That's how we learn new things and refine our process.

We also need feedback from others – not just any others, but what Ray Dalio in *Principles* described as "credible others". In other words, people who are knowledgeable and expert in the field and who will give you honest and reliable feedback. Dalio is the founder of Bridgewater, one of the most successful investment firms in the world. Dalio's notion of "credible others" appeals to me because you need to separate expert opinion from the rest. That way, you will not only be able to identify the useful information and the best sources, but you will also benefit from the expert feedback loop, which, research has shown, gets us closer to achieving excellence. Let me explain the feedback loop: you have an idea, your share your idea. Lots of people will willingly give their point of view, especially if it's a big idea, with a big impact on your life. That's feedback. You take on the feedback, act on it and have new, better ideas. People comment on your new ideas, you respond... that's a feedback loop. Ray Dalio makes the point that everyone has an opinion, and we must listen only to the opinions of those whom we believe to be experts. The rest is just "noise".

One can apply this principle of continuous process improvement to many aspects of life, but it's not always easy. I find the hardest stage of the 5-Step process is the final one: building your plan to achieve your goal. What often helps is to think about the processes you need to put in place and the reps that you need to do. When you set out to achieve something it can be exciting and motivating, and when you succeed the feeling of achievement is wonderful. Between those two peaks, however, there can often be a long stretch of time where you plod away, working at your process, improving it and following it, and it might seem that nothing much is happening.

The nature of change is that it's not linear. We sometimes plateau for a while and then suddenly make a big jump forward. That is why it's so important to note and record those small wins. It's also why you need to look back from time to time so that you can see the progress you have made. All too often we see only the mountains we have still to climb and we forget how far along the road we have travelled.

One of my closest friends is the journalist Sophie Kevany. We have known each other since the age of nine when we found ourselves in the same class in school. She helped me with the editing of this book and on reading this section she reminded me of the days when we were still schoolgirls and she and her father used to go walking in the Wicklow mountains. They would walk for four or five hours at a time in all weathers. On a fine day, Ireland is one of the loveliest places on earth, and the Wicklow mountains one of the loveliest parts of the country. The problem with Ireland is that a fine day is a rare day. Walking in the howling wind, with the misty rain coming down sideways into their faces, John would stop a moment and get Sophie to turn and look behind. "Before we climb the next peak", he would say, "just take a moment to see how far we have come". Sophie, all of 16 years old, would look back, note just how far they had come along the peaks and valleys of those granite-topped hills, then straighten her back and prepare to march forward.

Support yourself on the journey by taking the time to think about how far you have come.

Focus

❦

My business partner is Andrew Woodburn, Managing Director of South Africa's leading boutique executive search firm. Amrop Woodburn Mann competes in the African market with big executive search firms (popularly known as "headhunters") like Spencer Stuart and Heidrick & Struggles. In 2018 Andrew and I set up a new business, the Woodburn Mann Leadership Science Institute. We offer a range of leadership services to CEOs and Boards across the African continent. Or, as we like to say, "We bring the science of leadership to the boardrooms of Africa".

In the process of discussing how we would work together I came to know Andrew quite well. He is a high energy, intense individual who talks a lot. I don't know if I could have partnered with him a few years ago because I used to talk a lot too. Older now, and possibly a little wiser, I know that Andrew's intensity is his way of processing facts and situations, and that he needs that talking space in order to think. I'm comfortable to give it to him.

When Andrew meets someone, he zooms in on exactly what he needs from them. I mean that in a positive way. People come to headhunters with a purpose; either because they need to find a great executive or they want to talk about a job opportunity.

They expect the headhunter's full attention. It's incredible to watch Andrew do this with a possible candidate. As he talks to them, his mind is picking up on everything they say and do, putting those pieces together with what he already knows about that person, what's on their CV, what the research team has told him and what any third parties might have said. When the executive leaves the room and you ask Andrew what he thought, he will give a concise summary of exactly why they will fit a role, or not. In listening to him, a neutral person in the room who had never been involved in search would ask, "How did you get all that information from the conversation I just witnessed, and draw those conclusions?"

Like all great headhunters, Andrew does it because over the years his mind has become ever more attuned to what lies behind the responses given by each and every candidate. This is true expertise, one that takes time to develop and refine. It is the businessperson's version of the 10,000 hours in the context of executive search. You have probably heard of Malcolm Gladwell's idea that to achieve excellence in any field of endeavour, you must put in at least 10,000 hours of practice. I've chosen an example from my own world of leadership advisory and executive search, to show how experience and knowledge combine to enhance focus and allow seamless, rapid processing. I suspect that all great leaders do this, consciously and unconsciously, joining the dots to form a comprehensive picture.

Pieter Engelbrecht, CEO of Shoprite Holdings, one of South Africa's largest companies, once used an image for this that has stuck in my mind ever since. Shortly after he stepped into the CEO role, someone asked him what it was like. "Let me explain", he told me:

> It's like when you walk into a room you've never been in before, your mind instantly processes all the data, the floor colouring, the size of the windows, the red chair in the corner, the type of lighting, the flowers, the people in the room. If you tried to describe it all it would take an age but your mind takes it in an instant. This job is the same; there is so much information and data to process and my mind just does it at great speed.

The years of senior leadership that led up to his appointment as CEO have enabled Pieter to constantly process at this speed, taking everything in, joining the dots, and keeping his focus on what is important.

This ability is described by Daniel Goleman, one of the world's foremost writers on leadership and excellence. He coined the term '*Emotional Intelligence*' in his book of the same name. A few years later he wrote another fundamentally important work, *Social Intelligence*. In 2013, Goleman turned his attention to *Focus, The Hidden Driver of Excellence*.

Focus takes the concept of the 10,000 hours of practice a step further by suggesting that to become an expert, you have to focus on the right things. That means directing your attention, deciding what you want and then using a laser-like focus to achieve it. This is what Andrew Woodburn does. His mind filters the information he hears, like a brilliant tennis player lining up a great shot, without allowing conscious thought to interrupt the process. He has trained his mind to focus on what it is about this person that will make them a perfect fit for a particular role.

Taking Malcolm Gladwell's 10,000 hours a step further, Geoff Colvin published a book called *Talent is Overrated* in the same year. It is not that you need 10,000 hours of practice, he said, it's that your practice needs to be deliberate, disciplined and well designed in order to focus on the areas that need improvement. Goleman built on this again when he wrote about focus, pointing out that the mind literally trains itself to notice what we focus on, so the improvements become hard wired in our brains.

If that sounds like hard work, you're right, it is. Yet learning and growing are among the most rewarding of human accomplishments, particularly when we stretch ourselves.

There is a famous study which found that happiness comes from social connection and not from financial reward. Money is important though, and not having enough causes misery, not happiness. In the early 2000s, the happiness barrier was placed at USD75,000 a year. Less than that, life is too hard. But once you have enough, you don't get happier by having more. This aspect of the study is much reported.

What is less reported from the same study is its findings on satisfaction. Satisfaction and happiness are not the same thing. It turns out that the more successful you are, and the more money you make, the more satisfying you find your life. This is an unpalatable truth for many people, which is why it received less attention than the happiness quotient. We don't always want to believe that people are more satisfied with themselves and their lives because they have been more successful than others. It is true though, and this is why it's worth investing in learning, growth, finding your dreams, and making them reality. There is every chance that increased success will bring increased satisfaction.

No matter what you want to achieve, growing your knowledge and becoming an expert is one of the keys to success. The greater your understanding of a particular area, the better you will be at honing your mind to focus on what really matters.

Different tasks require different kinds of focus. When I started my academic research at the beginning of 2017 I was a complete novice. As I read through the work of previous students, I had absolutely no idea how I could possibly accomplish a finished thesis.

Determined to succeed, I did some research on thesis writing, created a plan and committed to it with absolute focus. I love reading books about mountain climbing and equated it to the effort required to summit a Himalayan peak. I estimated the number of hours I thought it would take on a monthly basis and then made sure I did those hours. When I felt fresh and confident, I did the writing. If I didn't feel like writing, I would read, find new articles, or research where I might find the articles that I needed. In research, there are always plenty of tasks that need to be done beyond the actual writing. This is mainly because academic writing requires the student to show how they did their work and why they took the decisions they did. My commitment to the process ensured that despite some unexpected disruptions, I got to the end and submitted on time.

I've since shared this concept of focus with my clients and some of them have really benefitted. Melinda (not her real name) is a good example of how changing your focus can help bring about transformation in leadership. She was moving to a new job and was really excited about the possibility of a fresh start. She is a communications expert, hard-working and highly skilled, but she has not always been good at building the professional relationships and network she needs in order to be successful.

When she moved into her new job we discussed how she might focus a little less on the technical aspects of her work – as a genuine and experienced expert she could accomplish that with less effort. Instead, she needed to focus on building relationships with her stakeholders, right from the start. That involved some of the skills that Goleman described in *Social Intelligence*, such as thinking about other people's motivations, putting herself in their shoes, and taking responsibility not only for the message, but also for how it lands and how it influences the behaviour of others.

Getting Melinda to shift her focus immediately helped her to build better relationships. Where she previously thought that managing stakeholders was something that got in the way of her work, she now sees it as a critical part of it.

Understanding that your focus will change as your career progresses is part of the challenge.

In Melinda's case, the first 15 years of her career involved building the technical expertise that now makes her one of the most trusted communications experts in her world. Her success saw her assigned a leadership role where she needed to delegate and deliver through others and engage more broadly with peers, something she initially struggled with. Bringing that aspect of leadership to her attention and changing her focus helped immediately.

In my career as an executive search consultant, and in executive assessments, I've seen this happen many times. We build our careers, like Melinda did, by developing valuable skills and knowledge, which we grow as our careers progress. For many people this is enough to get them to a middle, or even senior, management position by their late 30s or early 40s.

Stepping up to the next level requires new skills – most often the social intelligence ones sometimes referred to as "people skills". This is principally because the range of stakeholders with whom you need to engage has broadened considerably. Your relationship with your peers matters more at this level too, because you need to get things done as a team of equals, not just by yourself. At the same time, you need to ensure that those who report to you, often with strong ideas and opinions of their own, deliver. That means instead of telling them what to do, you need to understand how to motivate and inspire them.

Because we are social beings, understanding social intelligence is a key step to being successful in many aspects of life. Social intelligence is not about being popular and easy going, though those attributes may help. You don't need to be an extrovert to have high social intelligence. In fact, I've observed that extroverts can sometimes be lower in social intelligence than introverts, though I've not yet seen a study that backs that up. Social intelligence is about your ability to read other people and then flex your own style to get the best out of any interaction with them. As I described above when talking about Melinda, developing sophisticated social intelligence skills also means considering how your message will land with the other person and how it will impact their behaviour.

A broad focus can be a good thing

Does this mean you have to zone in on specific issues and focus on one thing at a time? Not necessarily. Some people are successful because they can manage a lot of different moving parts at once. I'm not talking about multi-tasking, which has been proven not to exist – it turns out that not even women can really multi-task.

Instead, I am talking about different kinds of intelligence, and we can improve our intelligence because we know our brain can be trained and grow. Think about this: world class CEOs and world class university professors are both extremely clever groups of people. The difference is that where the CEO is broad, the professor is deep. The way they focus is completely different. The CEO has to deal with constant change and complexity. They have to manage stakeholders, think strategically about the future and recruit a team of stars, while delivering immediate results. The professor will rather build a reputation on becoming an expert on one thing, often in a way that is difficult for the rest of the world to understand.

When my stepson, Christopher, submitted his PhD thesis in biotechnology to the University of Cambridge, I thought I should read it, even if I did not understand much. I didn't even understand a single sentence. My respect for Christopher grew exponentially. He had undertaken an in-depth study of a highly technical topic, going far beyond the layman's ability to follow. A CEO cannot do that. Instead, a key part of her job is to create followership. No matter how complex things are, she has to communicate what she is doing and bring people with her.

There are good examples of what a broad focus can do in sporting situations too. My eventing success is a case in point, as it is somewhat at odds with the amount of time and talent that I bring to it. I'm justifiably humble about my riding talent. I'm the wrong shape and my hand-eye coordination – so important when jumping – is not very good. I've spent far more of the past 30 years on planes, in meetings and in front of screens than I have on a horse. Yet when I compete I stand a fair chance of being placed in the top five at provincial and national levels. Not always, maybe not even often, but every year I get placed a few times and win once or twice, beating people who devote far more time to the sport.

Learning about focus has made me realise that it's precisely because I have the ability to keep several different priorities in mind at the same time, that I can do well. I relish the complexity: the planning, the training in multiple disciplines, the need to ensure the horse is fit and ready to compete, the constant interaction with farriers, vets, physios, feed merchants, trainers and a host of others, all suits my personality. That means, when I finally ride into the ring or jump out of the cross country starting box, I'm as well prepared as I can be and so is my horse.

The combination of focus and process is a winning one. Going back to what James Kerr said about the All Blacks in *Legacy*: if you identify what you need to improve, you have defined your focus and you can set goals accordingly. Then you can identify the processes you need to put in place to achieve those goals. Sounds simple enough, but it's hard to do, and that is where the 5-Step process can help.

When people struggle to do the 5-Step process it's usually the third step that is trickiest. That is when you choose three themes from your life and do a really deep, very personal brainstorm around each theme. Why do they struggle? I've thought about this a lot. Perhaps it's because choosing a theme may mean restricting your success in other areas. This reluctance to commit to doing a few things exceptionally well becomes obvious when I do the exercise with teams, so I suspect it also comes into play when you go through the process on your own.

Everyone has a dream or had a dream once. When you get to that third step, think about that dream. Are you on the road to achieving it? If yes, then you'll be able to do a great job on Step 3 and you will find working on it really invigorating.

If you once had a dream but you've lost sight of it, that's ok. That might even be why you're reading this book, which is a great step in the right direction. If so, I would say two things to you. Think really hard when you go through Steps 1 and 2. Take account of your whole person. Your dreams may have changed in a good way. Perhaps you wanted to be a rock star as a kid and now you're a hardworking man or woman with a family. Perhaps becoming a rock star was never a realistic dream anyway, as you didn't have a guitar, know how to play music or even sing particularly well.

As adults we are responsible for attaching our dreams to talents and skills we actually have; kids don't have to do that. When I talk about "dreams" I'm also talking about life as a responsible adult, so it's quite alright to have a theme like "spending more time with the kids" as your top priority. In fact, that is a great one, because wanting to leave in time for supper with them could make you tighten your focus at work. As a dream it may not be grandiose at first glance, but it's something that could change your future because of its impact on several different aspects of your life: your relationship with your children, your work rate and even beyond. As a coach I've worked with many clients on work-life balance and I encourage people to work smarter, not harder. Most of us can work smarter if we try and the outcome is often that we feel better and save ourselves time, while others notice the improvement in our working habits.

Choosing your focus is the key to success.

Information and Knowledge

❧

Whatever you decide to focus on, you will need to invest in expanding your knowledge in order to get the best possible results. No matter what your goals are, whether they revolve around business, sport, parenting or artistic endeavours, you will find there is a wealth of information that can help you. Sometimes you need to seek the information and sometimes others bring it to you.

A major theme that emerged from my MPhil research was that coaches bring new information to their clients, and that new information often leads to insights. Before they even think about providing any information, coaches listen to their clients. In fact, coaching may be the one place in the world, other than therapy, where people truly listen to your story and help you identify your needs. When a coach shares an idea with you, it's because they have understood what might help you. That is invaluable for clients, because not only is it coming from a store of expert knowledge on management, leadership and life, it's coming at the right moment when the client is open to hearing it.

In case any coaches are reading this book, I'm aware that a purist form of coaching would assert that the client already knows everything they need to know in order to thrive and move past their limiting assumptions. I don't hold strong views either way, but in field research on the coaching process it is clear that coaches often bring important information to their clients which helps their thinking process. That is what the first section of the book is about – sharing a few of the challenges that come up again and again in coaching, along with information that can help readers overcome them.

The important thing in coaching is that the client does the thinking and has the insight – and the coach is the catalyst for that.

If you don't have a coach, you can still extend your sources of information and there are suggestions for that in the appendix. To achieve your goals you will probably need to expand your knowledge. If you work in the corporate world and you aspire to a senior leadership role, what do you know about leadership? Just because you have an MBA and 15 years of experience, it doesn't necessarily follow that you are a great leader. Are you following current thinking on leadership and the skills and attributes of today's great leaders? Do you know what those skills and attributes are and how you stack up against global standards? Or how to develop and integrate them with your own skills and experience? That is the topic of my next book, not this one, but in the meantime, the reading list at the end is a good place to start.

Sometimes, what a client needs is the encouragement to dig down and find the information for themselves, and the coach needs to let them do their own research and thinking and not give them too much help. Isaac's story (not his real name) is a good illustration. We were talking about his frustrations in life and he said, "You know the worst thing is, Sarah, I'm a procrastinator. I want to do things, but I just cannot get started".

As it happens, I'm a procrastinator too, although I've worked hard to address the problem. There are a lot of procrastinators out there; you might even be one yourself. Because I've had to work on it, I know quite a lot about procrastination, but I didn't tell Isaac that. Instead, I asked him, "What have you done about it?" Isaac's answer was, "Nothing". "You mean you've got this big problem that you know is holding you back, and you've never done anything about it?" "That's right."

I set Isaac some homework. I suggested he look up procrastination on the internet, learn as much as he could about it, and ways of handling it, and then we could discuss his findings. "How did you get on with the research?" I asked at the next session. "I couldn't do it", he replied. "I couldn't get started."

There does have to be some spark of motivation if you want to change your life. If you have time to watch TV, scroll through Facebook or read a book, then you have time to research whatever is holding you back. The point is that although procrastination is a difficult and genuine condition, it can be addressed. If you suspect you are a procrastinator and you have not addressed it, perhaps you could set that as a theme for the year. Then research it, understand it and do something about it.

The motivation to get started on that research, to simply google the word "procrastination", is the first step out of that black hole. And that is precisely why I'm not giving you any answers here.

Often, coaches just ask the right question. Such as: "Do you procrastinate?"

Learning as adults

❧

Adults in the modern world cannot afford to stop learning; even if you have a business degree or an MBA, you can never stop learning about leadership and management. There are two reasons for this. First, because classroom learning can only touch the surface of such a deep, complex topic. The second is that the body of knowledge on these topics grows and improves all the time. You might not be in a senior leadership position until 10 years after your MBA, and if you did your MBA in 2007, the concept of emotional intelligence and its importance for leaders was only emerging. Social intelligence came even later. That means, unless you've done extensive reading in the last 10 years, you probably don't know nearly enough about either topic.

There are two famous models for adult learning. The first is the notion that we move from unconscious incompetence to unconscious competence. There's now stacks of research from both neuroscience and behavioural economics that explains how this happens, but the model itself is delightfully simple and resonates with most people.

Figure 3: Competency learning model

The classic example is that of learning to drive a car which almost everyone in the developed world does as a young adult. When you first get into a car you have no idea how to drive the thing. That is unconscious incompetence, when you don't even know what you don't know. Most of us then get started and crash a lot of gears, feel nervous on the road, struggle to coordinate everything and feel very clumsy. That is conscious incompetence. With practice (reps!) you become much smoother; you still have to think about what you are doing and concentrate, but you start to find driving quite easy. That is conscious competence. Then at some point, you arrive at your destination and thinking back you realise you can barely remember the driving; it was automatic. That is unconscious competence.

Most of us can achieve unconscious competence in many things if we work hard enough to understand what is required and then do the reps. What is much harder, is taking it to another level and becoming really good. That is where the 10,000 hours combined with lots of focus, good feedback and training comes in.

I was driving my horse to a competition in Port Elizabeth, 10 hours from Cape Town, and gave a lift to a friend called Sarah Yeo. Sarah was a new friend and I didn't know her very well. I had not really thought about her skills beyond equestrianism. I love how people surprise you. We shared the driving and when she got behind the wheel I instantly realised that she is a very good driver. I don't think I'm a bad driver and I'm certainly confident with a horse trailer, but her driving was in a different class. I asked her about it.

"Oh, I worked for BMW marketing for years and did lots of advanced driving courses and raced a bit as well." Wow! I wasn't expecting that. It illustrated how taking everyday skills, like driving a car, to a new level requires intense training and a lot of practice, and then challenging the skills in a tough environment like racing. The minute she was behind the wheel, even of my pedestrian Toyota SUV towing a horse trailer, her competence shone through.

The second adult learning model is more complicated and even more valuable. I'll attempt to pique your curiosity by telling you a little bit about it, but it's a huge topic and there are many books that cover it in detail. If you hunger for them, you can find plenty of sources. The model I describe here was proposed by David Kolb in his classic book, *Experiential Learning*.

Kolb's idea is that we all go through the same process of learning, but we access it from different points, according to our learning style. I might be the kind of person who likes to jump in, try new things and learn from my mistakes. You might be the kind of person who really likes to understand all the theory and to know exactly how something works before you try it. It doesn't matter which kind of learner you are, because the process is circular and we all learn in the end. It does help to understand that people learn differently though, because that increases your social intelligence. If you understand that not everyone on your team will have the same learning style, it will make you more tolerant of the person who seems reluctant to try something new. Maybe they need more information and understanding, and when they have that, they will be only too happy to try something they've never done before.

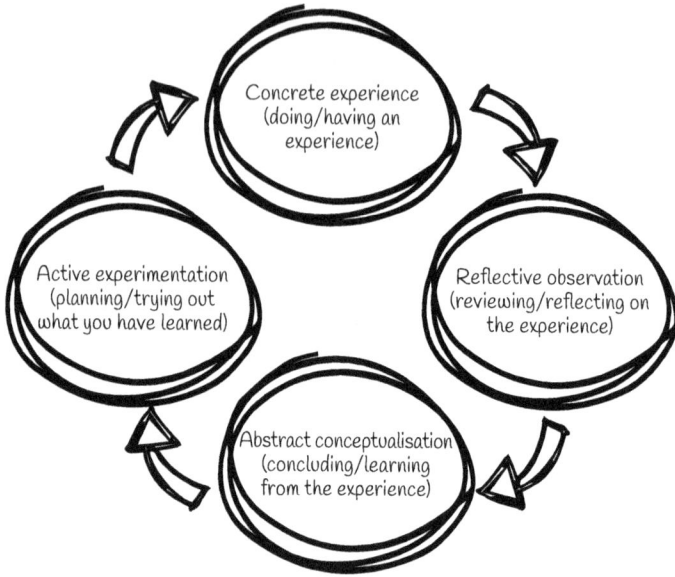

Figure 4: Kolb's learning cycle

Kolb's central idea is that "learning is the process whereby knowledge is created through the transformation of experience". Doing is part of adult learning and it really points to why it's ok to make mistakes, as long as we learn from them. Mistakes should encourage us to reflect on the experience, rather than hide from the opportunity to create new knowledge.

In *Black Box Thinking*, Matthew Syed describes the terrible experience of Martin Bromiley, whose wife died during a routine medical procedure. The hospital was genuinely sympathetic to the family, who were told that "something went wrong with the anaesthesia. These things happen". When Bromiley asked if there would be an investigation he was told there would not: "unless you sue." Doctors are not supposed to make mistakes and medical procedures are not meant to go wrong. When they do and people die, instead of doing a forensic investigation of the incident, the doctors and nurses call the time of death, mourn the tragedy, and move on.

Bromiley came from the airline industry. As you are surely aware, when planes crash they leave behind a "black box". This records everything that takes place in the cockpit during the flight. The actions of the pilots, the autopilot, what they said to one another, and the radio communications. If the plane goes down and the black box is recovered, it's given to investigators. Unlike medical accidents, plane crashes are always investigated. Not only are the accidents investigated, but any learning from that investigation is incorporated into airline procedures and shared with pilots worldwide. The power of the system is incredible, and thousands of lives have been saved because of the aviation industry's ability to address mistakes and learn from them.

Martin Bromiley did not sue the hospital, but he was determined that an enquiry should be held as to the cause of his wife's death. As a result of his persistence an investigation was commissioned, headed up by Michael Harmer, professor of Anaesthetics and Intensive Care Medicine at Cardiff University School of Medicine. The investigation found human error was at fault, and part of the problem was a combination of hierarchy and panic. The report made several key recommendations, and thanks to Bromiley's persistence, surgical procedures have been changed in hospitals throughout the world and many lives have been saved.

If this story, extreme as it is, resonates with you, it's worth thinking about how you respond to mistakes and feedback. Seeing both as a learning opportunity can greatly improve your work, as well as that of your team if you have one. Resistance to learning is often a sign of insecurity, as in the medical profession. If you find it hard to hear constructive feedback then you might think about where your insecurity comes from and what you can do to address it.

Understanding your own learning style is helpful and there's a useful questionnaire for this. If you look up 'Kolb learning style' online you will easily find a shortened version of it, although the full assessment should be administered by someone who is qualified to put the scores into context.

Once you realise that you can, and need to, learn more, all you have to do is to decide what to learn. Sometimes it's from experience and sometimes it's from mistakes. Often, it's from observing the behaviour of others, both good and bad. You can also learn a lot from books, and I have a few suggestions to get you started in the appendix section at the end.

People are different

❧

Emotional intelligence as a concept has received a lot of attention. Daniel Goleman, the man who coined the term, went on to write about social intelligence, "which, although every bit as important in any situation that involves people, teams and leadership" has less mainstream awareness. Now, however, academic research on social intelligence is starting to throw up some remarkable results. These help explain the impact we have on each other, and how we can use social intelligence to motivate ourselves and enjoy our lives more.

From a business perspective, social intelligence is probably the most important quality of senior leaders; more important than pure IQ and perhaps more important than emotional intelligence. Let me give you an example.

While I was President of Western Cape Eventing, one of the things we did as a committee was to bring inspiring world leaders to Cape Town to coach our riders, coaches, and officials. This initiative ended up having a much greater impact than expected. Not only did it inspire the riders and their coaches, but it brought the coaches together on a regular basis, away from the pressure of competitions. They got to know each other better and to understand each person's different strengths and weaknesses.

Because they were now helping each other as athletes, coaches and people, their teamwork improved. The wider impact of all those learnings, adaptations and improvements was that our province became unbeatable in national competitions. One of our top riders and coaches, Inge Silen, made a comment that really resonated with me. She said, "With this kind of exposure, we may be far from Johannesburg, but we feel very close to the rest of the world". Today, the international best practices we learned from that initiative are now part of how we train, how we build fences and how our officials operate.

In 2014 we were working on a project to establish the beautiful Kurland Hotel and Polo Estate as a potential venue for the South African Championships. The Fédération Équestre Internationale (FEI), which manages equestrian sports globally, advised us that Eric Winter, one of the world's top course designers and trainers, might be willing to help us. Eric is based in the UK and we had no funds to bring him to South Africa, but a generous friend of the sport contributed her air miles, and the necessary cash, to bring Eric over. That first step led to many benefits. Eric came to Cape Town for the first time in November 2014. He helped design the cross country tracks at Kurland in Plettenberg Bay and he spent two days training our officials. He now comes to South Africa twice a year and has become a great friend.

From that first experience I realised that Eric is a quiet genius – he is humble too, so he is not going to like reading those words. He is a consummate horseman and can train people in many dimensions, but his primary focus is cross country course design. He never stops learning, growing and trying new things. In 2017 he was asked to be the course designer for the Badminton Horse Trials, the global pinnacle of eventing competitions. Despite attaining these lofty heights, he still comes down to work with us. That is partly because he enjoys the good weather here in February, but mostly because he recognises our desire to learn, improve, and raise our standards.

Eric doesn't need to be the centre of attention and I've often noticed that he will sit quietly, out of the limelight, observing what is going on. He is the embodiment of one of my favourite sayings: "We have two ears and one mouth, and we should use them in that proportion." There's always a lot of politics around horses, for all sorts of reasons. Because he is both kind and thoughtful, Eric manages to avoid becoming embroiled himself, but at the same time he is willing to help those who are, to better navigate those tricky waters. Eric has unusually high social intelligence. He has deep insight into what people are like, and instead of being judgemental or expecting them to change, he uses that insight to help them improve in multiple areas. This, more than all his talent, may well be why he has achieved so much in his career. I learn a huge amount every time I work with him and I'm always humbled, because he reminds me, through his actions not his words, that I still have a long way to go in terms of my own social intelligence.

This is important to me because so much of what I want to achieve can only be realised with the support and help of others – my family, my friends and my colleagues. That's probably true for you too. So investing in a better understanding of how different we are from each other can help us to achieve our goals.

In fact, social intelligence, a vast, fascinating and complex topic, starts with that simple premise: people are different. When we evaluate senior executives one of the key attributes that we assess is social intelligence, and we look at it from many angles. You would be surprised how often senior executives, even CEOs, don't take this seriously, meaning they have never considered their own level of social intelligence, nor how they might improve. Yet the more senior you are as a leader, the more important it becomes.

My MPhil research involved talking with focus groups of experienced coaches about that magical moment of insight in coaching, the "Aha!" moment. My goal was to find out whether we could use the findings about decision-making that come from behavioural economics as a theoretical framework for coaching. Research already suggested that this approach, called dual processing theory, can help describe what happens in moments of creativity or insight. That meant it might help us to understand what happens in moments of coaching insight.

The coaches in my focus groups were all experienced business coaches, mostly working with people in the corporate world. As a student of social intelligence for many years, I was not surprised when the discussion revealed that a frequent client insight during coaching sessions is the realisation that people are different. Many clients have never even considered the idea that other people might be different from them, and that they think differently about life and work. To use a simple example, one of the coaches said:

> "When you wash your dishes, you wash them differently to the way that I would wash them. That's how intricate it is. Our rules of life are not the same. So, in every conversation people need to seek to be heard and also to listen to others, rather than assuming that because this is how I do it then everybody else does it the same way. And that there is no right or wrong way to do it."

Of course, we all believe that our way of washing the dishes is the best way, and I confess that I've never done a survey to identify international best practices in the daily task of dishwashing. I guarantee you one thing, though: the way I do it is not identical to the way that you do it. Now apply that to the many other "rules of life" and consider how different we all are, and then you will realise that social intelligence is basically about seeking to understand those differences and using them to improve communications with others.

How can you improve your social intelligence? The first thing to do is to focus on it, to think about the people around you, to try to spot ways in which they think differently to you, and to observe how they handle complex situations. Is it different to what you would have done? And was the outcome successful? Seek to identify the people who get the good outcomes and learn from them. In the business world you can probably identify which colleagues or leaders around you are good at smoothing over a meeting or handling awkward people adeptly.

If you're keen to improve your social intelligence I have two suggestions. One is that you observe those kinds of people – what they do, what they say and how they say it. The second suggestion is that when you have a sensitive situation that you need to handle, go to a colleague, a peer or a mentor that you trust, describe the situation, explain how you were thinking of handling it and ask them what they would do. What options do they see? As discussed earlier, we often get stuck in binary choices. But, like washing the dishes, handling difficult interpersonal situations, such as office politics, can be done in many different ways. Becoming a student of those possibilities will help you to develop your social intelligence.

Humility

❦

've already talked about humility as a pre-requisite for adult learning. Humility is the first topic in James Kerr's *Legacy*. In the first chapter we learn that the All Blacks clean up the changing rooms after themselves. Even after a great victory in their home stadium, you will find the superstars of New Zealand rugby "sweeping the sheds".

That story had a profound impact on me because it was the moment when I realised that humility and confidence are inextricably linked. To be truly confident one also needs to be truly humble, and one cannot be humble without a certain level of confidence. One of my own most powerful journeys in the past two years has been to identify and try to develop genuine humility; that journey began with *Legacy*. Along with Dr Steve Peters' *The Chimp Paradox*, it's the book I recommend most often.

Lessons don't always come from books, bosses and teachers, however. They often come from clients. When I asked Themba (a pseudonym that covers several client stories) to tell me about his life, he started by talking about Pretoria University. "No", I said. "I like to start at the beginning. Where were you born?"

So Themba told me he was born in a suburb of Johannesburg called Sophiatown. When he was still a child, the Group Areas

Development Act, 1955 came into force, preventing black South Africans from living in "white" designated areas. His home was bulldozed in front of the family's eyes to ensure that they would never return and they were moved to a black township.

Themba's father had a good job as a driver in Sophiatown, but he couldn't find work in the new township. Eventually, he went to work in the mines, leaving his family behind. Themba says his mother struggled with his absence and with how to raise a large family on the money he sent home. She did her best but the boys ran wild and started getting into trouble.

"How many brothers and sisters do you have?", I asked. "Six", he replied. "And what are they doing now?" "Eish. There were four boys and two girls. My older brother has had problems all his life. I still help him. He drinks and it's very hard for him. I came next and I was able to help the others. My younger brothers have done alright. The next one is an accountant, a senior manager now, and the youngest is an engineer. I am very proud of them. My sisters were different. One is married with her own kids, but she struggles. The other is a schoolteacher with a family. Her husband has done very well, he's an executive at Sasol."

"And what about your mother? Is she still alive?"

"Oh yes."

"She must be very proud of you?"

"Oh, she is, she is proud of all of us. We have bought her a house and I visit her often."

"And your father?" "He died while he was working on the mines. We think it was HIV/Aids, but we cannot be sure. After he died things got very hard for us. I started working, doing anything I could, when I was 12. And in a way, that's what saved me. My mother got a job as a domestic worker and I worked as a garden boy for her employer. But he told me he would only employ me if I did well at school and he helped me. Then I found a study group in the township on a Saturday morning. My mother's employer said I could go and he would still pay me, as long as I came to help in the garden in the afternoon. I learned a lot from that. Hard work, sure, but I also learned that not all rich people are bad. And that helping someone at the right time can change their life."

Themba is exceptionally bright. His school was not particularly good, but he still managed to get into engineering at university and was taken on by a large corporate when he graduated. He has never looked back. He supports the members of his expanding family and encourages the younger members to stay in school and work hard. "It's only a start, but it's the only start", he says.

I've heard many versions of this story during my years in South Africa. I'm amazed and humbled every single time. No-one in my privileged European world ever had to deal with anything like this, and with no help from the state, nor support from society.

What shines out from Themba's story is a lack of bitterness. Life dealt him a terrible hand as a child, yet he accepted every opportunity and nothing he said suggested he was jealous of those who got a better start in life. Sometimes, when I hear stories like these, full of grace and forgiveness, I don't know where to put the feelings I have. They are so full of hope for the future, I am not only humbled, I feel privileged to be the vessel that hears the tale.

On another occasion, I listened to a client describe how his personal success was tinged with sadness because he was unable to pull all his family along with him. At the end of the story our session was over and my client stood up. "I feel so much lighter", he said. "I don't think anyone has ever sat and listened to my story, like you have now." I was touched beyond words and we went on to build a wonderful coaching relationship, where both of us loved our sessions and we explored deep into the heart of things – of life, work, and family.

In my search for humility I learn most from my clients. In coaching we don't tell clients how to do things or how to improve. Instead, we walk along the road with them, for a few months or a few years as their confidante, their sounding board, their trusted advisor. As they open up their world and share concerns and challenges, we can only feel honoured to be part of that process, to understand how another human being thinks and feels, and how they strive to grow.

The role of coach is wonderful, endlessly challenging and deeply humbling.

Part Two – Commitment

"Integrity is the consistency of words and actions."

Kenneth Chenault

Chapter 10

Integrity

How do you define integrity? My main professional skill is assessing CEOs and other senior executives, often in the context of an executive search process or succession planning project. As part of that I am often asked to assess people's integrity. But what is integrity and how do you define it? I finally came across a definition that I like and it's very simple: integrity is doing what you say you'll do. Doesn't sound like much, does it? Many definitions of integrity are more high flying, such as this one: the quality of being honest and having strong moral principles; moral uprightness. In ethics studies, they say it's about the honesty and truthfulness or accuracy of one's actions. I like that one better, but I still prefer: doing what you say you're going to do. Imagine a world where everyone aligned their actions and their words? Imagine a business where everyone delivered on what they said they would do? What a transformed world we would live in.

I don't think I've ever met anyone who doesn't claim, sincerely, to have integrity, but too often their words and actions don't meet up; there's a gap between our idea of ourselves and the reality of how we show up in the world. We mean well, but we don't always deliver.

Writing about integrity reminded me of a personal story that demonstrates why it matters.

I lost my mother when I was very young. Things that are connected to her are unusually important to me. One day, I was chatting to a friend of hers who told me that before I was born, she was at my mother's house and admired a picture on the wall. As she was leaving, my mother gave it to her. "That picture is in a cupboard now Sarah", she said, "I'll find it and give it to you".

For several years after that, whenever we met, she would mention the picture and that she was planning to give it to me. She never did, and now I know she never will.

It was the words "I'll give it to you", that created the expectation, and with that expectation came a whole lot of feelings. Whether or not I liked the picture, I would have hung it on the wall and every time I looked at it, I would have thought what a kind person my mother was, what lovely friends she had, and how much it meant that she was not forgotten.

This woman is deeply religious and was involved in politics for many years. She would certainly say of herself that she has great integrity, maybe even that integrity is one of her core values. She did not do what she repeatedly said she would do though. Her actions and her values were not aligned.

The reason I've shared such a personal story about integrity is because I want to stress the real meaning we attach to both words and actions, and how important it is that your words and actions are congruent, at the very least when you are making promises to yourself. In a world where US Presidential elections and UK referenda can be influenced by blatant lying, we may wonder whether integrity is a lost value. It's not for me to judge your choices. If you want to plan for success though, you'll need to commit to action and your actions need to reflect your commitment. Integrity is not just about doing what you've told someone else you'll do. Above all, integrity is about holding yourself to account and keeping your promises to yourself.

Take the words of Thuli Madonsela, one of the bravest women I have ever encountered. As South Africa's Public Protector she coined the phrase "state capture" to describe what was happening in South Africa under the leadership of President Jacob Zuma and his allies, the Gupta family. Madonsela has been fearless in her pursuit of justice for South African citizens and inspirational in her own right. She said: "We cannot lead others if we cannot lead ourselves. The hallmark of leadership is responsibility." This is one of the most important things we need to understand about leadership, because we must each be our own leader and shoulder that responsibility.

For responsibility read integrity. Make the commitment to yourself and then do what you say you are going to do. This is the first step in leadership.

In the next few chapters there are some tools and suggestions that should help you keep your self-leadership on track as you set out to achieve your goals. If you get stuck, you can come back to this section and see if there's an idea here that might help reset, reprioritise, or re-motivate you.

Chapter 11

Priorities

❧

Maybe it's not that you don't have a dream or an objective for the year... maybe you have too many. Some of my clients have found it difficult to do the 5-Step process because, as you will see when you get to Part Three, you have to choose themes; areas in your life you want to change. From those themes, you create your objectives. The clients who found it hard said they couldn't decide on just three life themes, nor three objectives per theme. You can have more themes of course, but if you choose three and then have three objectives per theme, that's already a lot of goals. If you succeed in achieving those you'll be very pleased with yourself. Indeed, I would challenge you to set bolder, bigger objectives, not more of them.

In short, go big and focus your efforts on a few important themes rather than scattering your efforts too widely.

In my own case there are parts of my life that require ongoing management, of myself or others, but they might not appear on my list of themes. They include sport, my weight, an Airbnb business, daily household and garden chores, and seeing friends. That's to say nothing of the annoying management of the minor health issues that crop up as one gets older. When I set my themes I try to think about the bigger picture. That's where Step 3 is so helpful, because it puts the focus on outcomes; on what will make you feel great six months or a year from now. At this point in my life my main focus is building a great business as well as promoting this book and working on the next one. My garden has been neglected and it might be a theme for another year. Understanding my priorities helps in another way too, by reducing frustration. So, for example, once I have accepted that gardening has to take second place to growing my business this year, I feel less frustrated by what I am not manging to do.

Don't think that your themes have to be world beating and awe-inspiring. Some years you might choose to focus on freeing up more time to spend with your kids or walk in the park once a week. You may want this to be the year you write a book, get a big promotion, or start a business. Or it might be the year where you devote more time to caring for an elderly relative and find a way to do it with grace and good humour. The point is to reflect on your life and spend time thinking about what you really want. If you do that, you will achieve more, and better, than you ever thought possible.

When you start the planning exercise, get some paper and a pen organised and find a quiet place where you can concentrate. When you're working on achieving your objectives throughout the year, remember the importance of focus and that we cannot multi-task. To get good results we need to concentrate.

How do you remember what to focus on as the year progresses? Keeping your priorities and objectives in mind is important, because in the everyday world we get interrupted by immediate urgencies. One of the best tools to help manage this is the Eisenhower Matrix. I first saw it in Stephen Covey's 7 *Habits of Highly Effective People* in the early 1990s, and I've been recommending it ever since.

Here's how it works. A lot of our time every day is spent doing urgent tasks that come up and demand attention **now**. Technology makes it even worse. Think of the 'ping!' that announces the arrival of an email, text, WhatsApp, Tweet or even a Facebook notification. The urgent desire to see what it says and respond immediately is similar to the kick you get from alcohol, drugs, chocolate or exercise. Your brain releases a little shot of dopamine in anticipation of pleasure.

That's not good because that means technology is addictive. You can't give up technology if you live in the real world, so the pressure of the 'ping!' adds to the stress of your everyday life. Other urgencies intrude on your world all the time. From the project that you haven't started because you were either "too busy" or procrastinating, to the sudden crisis that hits your department and means all hands on deck until it's resolved.

The Eisenhower Matrix suggests that you look at tasks in light of their importance and their urgency. We tend to enjoy doing urgent tasks because we get an adrenaline kick from them and it's satisfying to get them ticked off. That means we do the important and urgent tasks, but too often it also means we do tasks that are urgent, but not important. The ones that are neither urgent nor important tend to be the ones that drop to the bottom of your inbox and stay there until you eventually delete them (and that's ok, you could probably just have deleted them in the first place). The problem is that the *important but not urgent* tasks are the ones we tend to neglect, and that's why we miss our goals.

Doing the 5-Step processing exercise is all about *important but not urgent*. The outcome – the plan for the year – is in itself an important, but often not urgent, task. That is why focussing on it at the beginning of the year can be so helpful, because we are already attuned to things like New Year's resolutions and are ready for change. Even so, it can be hard to think deeply about your themes and then to do the work of building your goals and making your plans.

Understanding the Eisenhower Matrix and the value of figuring out which tasks are important but not urgent, and then investing time and focus in those tasks, could be one of the most powerful changes you make to your life.

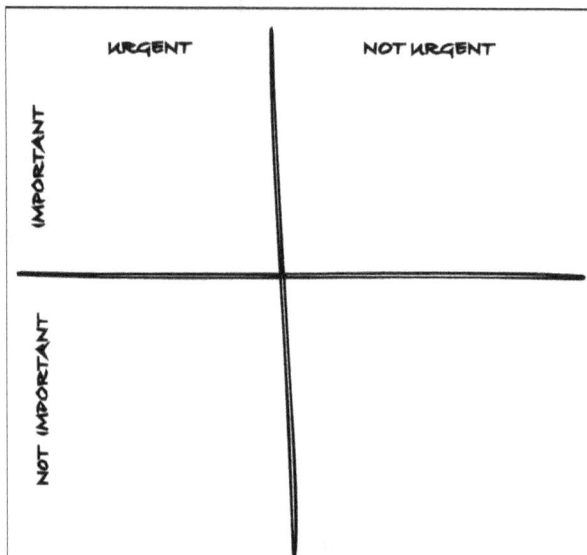

```
                URGENT          |        NOT URGENT
                                |
   I                            |
   M                            |
   P                            |
   O                            |
   R                            |
   T                            |
   A                            |
   N                            |
   T                            |
  _____|_____
   N                            |
   O                            |
   T                            |
                                |
   I                            |
   M                            |
   P                            |
   O                            |
   R                            |
   T                            |
   A                            |
   N                            |
   T                            |
```

Figure 5: The Eisenhower Matrix

Whether you are sorting tasks or implementing your plan, the Eisenhower Matrix will help you to prioritise. Keep it in front of you and make sure you put your long-term objectives from the 5-Step process into the *important not urgent* quadrant at the top right. As tasks come up, spend a moment allocating them to a box. If they are *urgent but unimportant*, think very carefully before you allocate time to them.

If they are neither important nor urgent you probably should not be doing them at all.

If they are urgent and important, meaning your house is on fire or you need to take someone to the emergency room, then you will not hesitate for a moment to prioritise that.

Here is how I use the matrix. I always have a To Do list on the go, and with a life made up of many parts, it's quite disconnected so it can be hard to prioritise properly. To illustrate the Eisenhower Matrix for you, I simply took my current To Do list off my phone.

To do list

Arrange compost delivery
Sort out London trip
Call Aunt Ann
Send documents to Ireland
Book Appt with Dr D
Tidy office
Sort out paperwork
Create new shopping list template
Work on presentation for KR
Write blog article for clients
Get book endorsements
Get Peter's phone fixed
Research new 360 profiling tools
Book equine dentist
Send Christopher the Power of Small Wins
Write up coaching sessions for the week
Prepare assessment pack for next week
Learn dressage test
Pack for show

Figure 6: To Do list

Then I put every item into the appropriate box on the matrix. If I saw something I could quickly sort out there and then, I did so. For example, I had been talking to my stepson Christopher about *The Power of Small Wins*, an article in the *Harvard Business Review* that I refer to in Chapter 2 and that I had promised to send him. Even though it was not important in the bigger picture of goals, I had promised it to him and I quickly sent it right away, crossing it off my To Do list. That probably took less than one minute.

This is how I assigned the items on the matrix.

	URGENT	NOT URGENT
IMPORTANT	Arrange compost delivery Send documents to Ireland Book Appt with Dr D Work on presentation for KR Prepare assessment pack for next week Learn dressage test Pack for show Pack for Monday	Sort out London trip Call Aunt Ann Write blog article for clients Get book endorsements Research new 360 profiling tools Write up coaching sessions for the week
NOT IMPORTANT	Send Christopher the Power of Small Wins	Tidy office Sort out paperwork Create new shopping list template

Figure 7: The Eisenhower Matrix filled in from my To Do list

The 'urgent and important' items needed doing that day. For example, why was compost urgent? Because in the Cape we plant in May and the soil needed to be prepared. I'm lucky to have a gardener to do that, but I needed to order the compost so that he could. Next, I was riding in a competition at the weekend and I had not learned the dressage test. That is not something I could leave until the very last minute because experience tells me my brain seems to need a couple of days to embed the sequence of movements so that I don't make a mistake on the day.

These things all needed to be actioned that day, no matter what.

The important not urgent items are the most interesting. These are more strategic or may carry deeper meaning. Many of the outcomes from the 5-Step process belong here. If you are a procrastinator you might never get to these items, yet they may be the ones that will change your life. In the case of this example, take "Write blog article for clients". I send my CEO coaching clients well researched and informative pieces that will be of interest to them. I started doing it because I realised they don't have much time to read articles on leadership, strategy and management. The topic ideas are usually triggered by something that came up in a session, so that they are pertinent and may inspire a new idea or line of thinking. This takes mental effort to do, and not being urgent, if it's not highlighted, it's something I could easily forget or procrastinate about.

Some items in this column are not urgent now but they will become urgent if I don't sort them out quickly. In this example, if I don't set up my meetings for a trip I've planned to the UK in a few weeks' time, I might lose out because the people I want to see may already be busy.

Talking about trips reminds me to share something I've learned over a lifetime of constant travel, which is to plan, and even pack, well in advance. Until quite recently I used to get caught up in my busy life and leave planning and packing to the last minute. Now I find I'm calmer and feel more organised if I plan several weeks in advance. If I find myself with some free time during a busy travel period I will even pack for trips that are several weeks away. This sometimes leads to a sense of adventure as I unpack, not being quite sure what's in my case. And I love the feeling of getting home from a busy day or a busy week and being able to have a glass of wine, some supper and an early night because the suitcase I need for the next day is standing there waiting for me, ready to go.

If you don't pay attention to items in the *important not urgent* column, one of two things will happen: either they will suddenly become urgent and you will end up doing them in a hurry and maybe not as well as you could, or if you don't do them, they slip away, never get done, and you move further and further from achieving your goals.

When I look at the *not important, urgent* items, they belonged there because they were not important to achieving my goals, but they were important in a different way. If I've promised Christopher I will send him an article, I need to do it.

Finally, the *not important, not urgent* items, like tidying my office and sorting out my paperwork. I'll get to that eventually, when I have a quiet moment. Some people are very tidy and organised about their offices. I'm not, and I've learned to live with it.

I hope that helps illustrate the point. You don't always have to lay your To Do list out in this matrix, but you should have a good sense about which quadrant in the matrix each item belongs to, because it will help you to focus and prioritise your actions.

Many of your outcomes from the 5-Step process belong in the *important not urgent* box. You might want to develop a system where you address these tasks first thing in the morning, before you get down to anything else. It might be that, like Colette in Chapter 1, you break everything down into smaller chunks to help identify where and how to move forward. Or you might use one of the productivity tools that I describe in Part Three.

Writing a big academic thesis involves months of work. When you are in the middle of it, it can seem like an impossible task. In this case, the Eisenhower Matrix doesn't help so much because every task is important and none is urgent. Academic work is hard, and there were times when it took me three hours to write three sentences. As a believer in process, I thought – why not apply it here and see what happens? I calculated roughly the number of hours it should take to write the thesis and broke that down into a certain number of hours per month. On a spreadsheet I ticked off the hours I worked, using the Pomodoro app (an alarm that helps you focus on one thing for 25 minutes and then take a break) to make sure I recorded only the hours spent doing actual research and project tasks.

I did not commit to a specific number of hours per day or per week, but I made sure I met my monthly targets. Other people might have chosen to stick to a daily or a weekly target; it depends how structured your life is. Then I broke the work down into easy, harder and really hard tasks. If I did not feel full of energy I would do an easy task, such as searching for relevant articles for example, or editing my previous work. If I was full of life and raring to go I would tackle the harder tasks of writing and research.

As long as I was in my chair and working on my thesis, I would tick off the hours. I took the view that it was like climbing a Himalayan summit: if I followed the process step-by-step, I would summit the mountain at the right time. And I did.

That achievement bolstered my conviction that success is about setting objectives and then identifying the best process to achieve that success. So, first step, identify the best possible outcomes, and then, second step, keep your focus on the process. By continually refining and improving the process, you will achieve better and better outcomes.

If you did this exercise last year and you find that your themes have not changed much, you might not see the point of setting new objectives. That's not a bad thing, but you might want to search for a fresh approach or a new process to help you implement your plan.

Take diet and weight, for example, which is a challenge for many people, myself included. Last year I said weight would be an absolute priority, and indeed, for most of the year I had it under control and was quite pleased. As the year came to an end a whole bunch of things happened that took my focus off my weight and suddenly I'm back where I started, but I don't see this as a failure.

In my case weight has been a lifelong challenge, so it's nothing new. But I do need to take another look at how I handle some aspects of my life, including travel, socialising, the odd crisis, family celebrations and so on, in order to identify a process that will help me maintain good habits even when I lose focus. Same theme, same objective, different process.

Going back to the Eisenhower Matrix, one of the problems with life is that just after you've taken some time over the New Year to create this fantastic plan, you go back to work. After the break, everything's crazy and all the super urgent things come crashing down on you demanding to be done *now*! The difference with using the 5-Step process is that you will have a clear idea of what's important for the longer term, and a path to steer toward that through all those immediate demands. Even then, however, it can sometimes be hard to ensure you get the important tasks done and stay focussed on achieving your goals.

Six things can help

Here's a tool that can help you with that.

It's called the "Six Things List" and it's a golden oldie. Before you go to bed each night you write a list of six things to do tomorrow. The next day you do them, before you do anything else. The six (or fewer) tasks should be listed in order of importance and every one of them should be important (see the Eisenhower Matrix above). When you're interrupted, as you will be, you compare the importance of the interruption with your six things. Unless it's more important, you continue with the six things until they're done.

Here are a few rules to help you:

Write the tasks on your list every evening, either before you leave the office or before you go to bed.

The things on the list must be important to you.

You must be able to complete each item on the list within the day. Remember, if you can't, it's too big and you need to break it down into more manageable tasks.

You complete the items on the list before you even look at the day's emails. That's quite a frightening thought, I know!

Write the list in order of importance and complete the list in that same order.

Commit to it. Do it every single day. Your productivity will soar. If you drop the habit, get back to it. It is so easy to do.

Change and choice

❦

When you jump a horse over fences you use hand-eye coordination to judge the right take-off point. Eric Winter describes it as "the shot". You can have a good shot or a bad shot. Like many things in riding horses this sounds simple, but in practice it's not easy. When you get it right it's a beautiful feeling. You and an animal that weighs about half a ton are in perfect sync, your bodies seamlessly meeting the five stages of the jump, landing and flowing forward again to the next fence. That's how it should go.

When you get it wrong, as everyone does from time to time, even the professionals, your body goes into panic mode. The clear communication between you and the horse is lost and the result is either an ugly jump or a stop. If the fence is big or the pace is fast the rider quite often falls off. When it goes well the horse is like an intelligent bouncy rubber ball as they approach the fence. As long as that communication is kept intact and the rider has a reasonable idea of a good take-off point, all she has to do is keep that connection secure and the horse can simply compress or extend their stride to reach that perfect point. When the rider is a professional, with hours and hours of training and jumping under their belt, they are usually just fine, but most riders are amateurs and don't have the time or the will to put in all those training hours. One of the challenges is that it feels much easier and safer to approach the fence slowly, but it's harder for the horse to jump if they aren't powering forward.

Getting better at managing the power and jumping cleanly is all about "reps", or the 10,000 hours. The more you do, the better you get.

The purpose of this is not to give you a lesson in show jumping, but to give you some context about a fall I had not too long ago and what I understood from it later. While I know the theory about not panicking when things go wrong, it's a lot harder when it's all actually happening. My horse Filipe is a big horse. I bought him when he was young because despite his size I thought we had a rapport and felt he was incredibly talented. I was right on both counts; we have a gorgeous relationship, we have won a lot of prizes and it has been a joyous journey.

One damp Monday, though, our journey temporarily went from joyful to painful. I was having a jumping lesson with my coach, Daniela Smit, known as Dan. We were starting to jump bigger fences and Dan had just put the fences up to 1.20m height. Anything at or above this height is a significant challenge for even the best horse and rider, and the barrier can be psychological as much as physical. Despite everything I've just said, all my training reps and knowledge, I came around the corner without enough power, could not see the shot, flapped my legs and Filipe took a huge leap into the air, twisting his big body to ensure that he cleared the fence. The problem was that three strides later there was another fence and I knew that we had no chance of clearing that. So, in mid-air I pulled on the rein to avoid the second fence. Bad mistake. He twisted some more, and I lost my balance and fell off. Ever since I broke my back I wear an air-jacket when I jump. When you fall it deploys and inflates before you hit the ground, protecting you from neck to hip. The trouble is when you wear an air-jacket you cannot tuck and roll in the same way that you would without one. On this occasion my jacket malfunctioned, the only time it has done so, and I fell hard onto my shoulder and arm.

One of the chapters I love in *Legacy* is the one about leaving blood on the field. Wounds sustained in the field of battle are honourable wounds and most often result from being outside your comfort zone; when you stretch yourself, as we were doing that day. If it goes wrong and you get hurt, it's an honourable injury.

That day I didn't have much time to think about it. I was flying to Geneva that night to see a client, and I had to get myself to the airport and onto the plane. As I waited to board my upper arm was throbbing horribly, so I nipped into the ladies to get a better look. I took off my jacket and rolled up my sleeve and everything was black and blue and swelling rapidly. The woman washing her hands beside me was horrified by the sight. After we boarded I sent a text to Dan. "Not looking great." "Remember", she replied, "It is not what happens to you but how you handle it that counts".

I couldn't put my bag up into the luggage compartment, but someone kindly helped me. My arm felt strange and didn't quite work. It was very painful, so I took an anti-inflammatory and had a stiff drink followed by a sleeping pill, breaking any number of rules. Finally I fell into a drugged sleep wondering if my arm might be fractured and what on earth I would do about that when I landed in London to catch the connection to Geneva the next morning.

Well, it was fine in the morning. Not fine exactly, the bruising and swelling took weeks to disappear, but it wasn't broken.

The reason I'm sharing this story is not to show you how tough I am, because I'm not. Rather it's to point out that because of choices I had made that day, I ended up in a position that was probably rather stupid: on an overnight flight with a potentially fractured arm. Sometimes people blame others for what happens to them and I could have blamed Dan for pushing me on a day when I was a bit stressed and off my game. Or the horse for doing something a bit silly (he did not, but riders often blame their horses for their own mistakes). Or even myself for agreeing to try something challenging at the wrong moment. But to be honest, the throbbing arm was the consequence of a series of choices I've been making all my life. Simply put, my current philosophy goes a bit like this: ride when you can; push yourself because jumping bigger fences is more challenging and ultimately more fun than jumping smaller ones; raise your game on your horse and at work; work hard at your job; never let the client down; always deliver.

Sometimes those choices are incompatible and end up meaning that where maybe I should go for an x-ray, I get on a plane. The longer term consequence of that particular choice was probably a slower healing process and definitely a lot more pain, but I did the work and delivered. Even better, I luckily had a long-sleeved shirt with me which covered the swollen, dark-blue bruising on my right arm when I sat in front of the client that hot June day in Geneva.

Most of all, I'll never forget what Dan said. "It is not what happens to you but how you handle it that counts." It's not the first time I've faced that kind of choice and decided to do the client work. We may not have much choice about the adversities that we face in life, but we do have choices about how we handle them. Dan and I have both been through periods of real grief in our lives and we have accepted the need to respond to loss, to mourn, and to suffer. I would not judge how any person responds to tragedy. However empathetic we are, I don't believe we can put ourselves in another's shoes when they lose someone they love.

Once the worst is over and it's time to pick up the reins of responsibility and life again, that's when the choices begin. At that point you have the opportunity to choose things that will create positive outcomes in your life. Yet how many people do you hear blaming others, or events, for their situation in life when in fact they most likely had an opportunity to choose a different path? "It's how you handle it that counts."

Think of Themba in Chapter 9. He grew up in a difficult environment where opportunities were extremely limited. He grasped every bit of luck and opportunity that came his way, consistently choosing a tougher path – to work and study as hard as he could. That grit defines him even now, and grit is one of the qualities that will help you to make good choices and taken on challenges.

If you want to achieve your dreams, grit will trump talent every time. In Chapter 5 I talked about how your practice needs to be deliberate, disciplined and designed to keep you focussed on the areas that need improvement. When you do the "reps", it's not just about putting the hours in, but about doing the right "reps" to take your performance to the next level.

> Exceptional people don't just do the work, they are really smart about what work they need to do.

Willpower

There are times when the choice is clear. To go to the gym, or to go home? To sit down and write the report now, or to do it at the last minute?

Sometimes you have more options than you realise. We saw that in Chapter 3, when I shared Jerome's story and explained how you can broaden your frame and create a wider range of choices. You can choose to push yourself when you run, so that every session makes you fitter and every sprint matters. Or you can stop. Or, here is a new choice, you can plod along, happy in the knowledge that any aerobic exercise, done three times a week for more than 20 minutes, leads to a longer and healthier life.

Perhaps more important than the type of choices is remembering that choice is an extraordinary gift, and something to which we should pay more attention. One of the primary benefits of planning and commitment is that we can make better, and ultimately more rewarding, choices.

If one of the important challenges you have set for this year involves change, whether at work or in your personal life, then you need to understand a bit about change and choice. As I mentioned earlier, it's important to focus on process when you are doing your planning. When you want to achieve something, big or small, you need to break it down into the tasks that will get you there and focus on accomplishing those, rather than on the finished product of the dream you want to achieve. That is because your dream is often too vast an achievement to think about every day and the daunting challenge could end up putting you off.

If you've never run a road race and you want to take part in a 10 kilometre event, you cannot start out by thinking about running 10 kilometres.

You start out with a plan that helps you understand what the best time of day is for you to run. How are you going to get yourself into your running shoes and out of the house on your running days? Do you need to supplement your running with other exercise like yoga or Pilates so that you increase your strength and decrease your risk of accidents? Classes might help motivate you.

Finally, you need a strategy that gets you from 0 – 10km in manageable chunks. The first day might be walking 100 paces and running 100 paces at intervals for 20 minutes. That would be a fantastic start. Focus on the steps and you build a ladder to your dream.

The same is true at work. If you decide you're going to aim for a big promotion this year, you need to understand what it will take to get that promotion and whether it's realistic in a year. The promotion is not really the aim, it's the outcome; the result.

The aim is to understand all the things you will need to do differently this year to convince your boss you're ready for that next level job. Things like showing up a bit differently at work, taking more ownership of your tasks, understanding more about the bigger picture of the business so that you can add more value in your role.

No matter how committed you are, it's important to know that when you need willpower to make good choices, cunning planning will be involved. Our daily ration of willpower is limited. This has been researched and we now know that the attrition of willpower during a day is the result of chemical changes in the brain's executive function. Every time you make the harder choice instead of the easier choice, you burn up a little bit of willpower. In the morning, when the brain is rested and fresh, it's easy to have fruit for breakfast, go to the gym or to start your most difficult project first. Although, if you're like me and not really a morning person, it's never exactly easy to do all that, but it certainly is easier in the morning than in the evening.

After a long day in the office, making good work choices and saying no to the bad food choices that presented themselves, you'll be tired and your executive function wants to make your choices easier. Unless you have a really good plan in place, you're going to find it much harder to resist that glass of wine or a piece of chocolate cake. Understanding this helps, because it helps you to realise that you're not a weak person – you're just a human being, like the rest of us. With a bit of planning, you can make those good evening choices easier.

Planning your choices

The 5-Step process helps you align your choices with your true values, which is grounding and builds confidence. Putting the process and focus in place to make sure you do the "reps" will help turn your good choices into good habits by automating them.

While I was researching this book I read a study that looked at how our social intelligence can help us make good choices. We are social beings and while we might not always make a great choice for ourselves, it's surprising how often we will do it to help someone else.

When we can associate our good choices with the pride that comes from delivering benefit to others, we make better choices. This is quite an extraordinary claim, but one that is supported by several scientific studies. Think of it this way – if you want to diet or to get fitter, and you can find a friend who wants to do the same but has less willpower than you do, you'll be more inclined to make good choices in order to help them. Or maybe that friend will help you. It works both ways. This is one reason groups work so well for setting and achieving objectives, not just because of the peer pressure, but because there's altruism involved, i.e. wanting to do something for the others.

> To put it simply, if you can harness your naturally altruistic inclinations to make better choices, you'll increase your chances of success.

You could add integrity to the mix: being true to yourself and your commitments, delivering every single time to the very best of your ability, not getting distracted by unimportant matters, not getting angry about things you have no control over. Instead, if you aspire to a leadership role, invest in your commitment by reading and understanding more about leadership. If a management role is what you're after, find out more about what is expected.

These goals will involve changing your habits in one way or another. If you're not in the habit of reading, you need to find time to do that. If you're not in the habit of sitting down and thinking about what the business expects you to deliver, and how you can deliver above and beyond expectations, you need to think about what must change for you to do that. If you get emotional or fly off the handle, or if you are not consistent in your dealings with colleagues, you need to do something about that too. If that's your challenge, I have a suggestion for you in the next chapter.

Thinking through your current habits and choices, as well as how you can better align them with your themes and your purpose, is a good way to start engaging with the changes you need to make.

None of this might seem easy, but keep your eyes on the main event. You have a dream. You make a plan. You take the steps. And here's an additional plus; as you set your themes and objectives using the 5 Steps, new, sometimes surprising, ideas and choices will often emerge as your world becomes less binary and more open to possibility.

When you're ready, decide what you need to do to achieve your plan, breaking it down into the smallest chunks you can. Commit to doing it, and, day by day, you will find you are making better choices – one aligned with your plan. You have integrity. You achieve your dream.

Self-management

❦

The first time I ever saw a grown man actually screaming at someone in a meeting room was more than 10 years ago in South Africa. The place was the Spencer Stuart offices in Johannesburg, and the man was (back then) a senior partner. I had known him for many years. We both held leadership roles in the firm and regularly met at international conferences when I was living in Paris and London. I had just moved to Johannesburg and was sitting in a staff meeting. One of the researchers, smart, opinionated, and good at her job, raised an objection to the approach the partner was suggesting and he lost it. He simply could not bear to have his authority questioned. Sadly, it was not the last time I was to see this kind of behaviour. People who might, on the surface, appear to be not only highly intelligent but also absolutely charming, can, the minute their will is crossed, go on the attack, vocally and sometimes quite aggressively.

Speaking from personal and professional experience, I would add, sadly, that this behaviour is more prevalent in South Africa, in work and sport, than anywhere else I've lived.

Given that my job involves assessing people from a range of backgrounds and cultures, I can also say with confidence that this behaviour is not limited to any particular culture. It occurs primarily in men, or perhaps the way in which women attack is different, quieter. I've also observed bad behaviour in women leaders, but it's less direct, noisy and aggressive.

The purpose of this book is not to discuss South African culture, but one can imagine that this behaviour reflects some of the deep-seated insecurity that remains at the heart of the nation. Whatever the cause, it has no place in the workplace. When I give motivational talks and work with large groups and teams, one of my aims is firstly to highlight this issue, and secondly, to help people understand that they don't need to behave this way. That self-management is important and possible, and that we will be richer and happier as a result.

I sympathise with the problem because my own biggest development area is a tendency to become emotional and to react too quickly. I've worked on my self-management over the years and I'm much improved, though pressure always tends to reveal one's weak spots. Consistency is one of my favourite management words and it's something I really apply to my own leadership. If you call me, no matter how I feel about the call, I will always endeavour to be pleasant, friendly and wanting to know how I can help you. That attitude seems to be a good starting point for most conversations.

Surprisingly, many people, even those in senior leadership roles, don't understand the concept of self-management. The concept of "authentic leadership" has not helped, because it's often misunderstood and hijacked to justify bad behaviour. If my bad behaviour is authentic, then it just means I am an authentic leader, says an executive to his coach. No, it does not. It means you are both selfish and lazy, because you have not invested the necessary time and energy to understand either leadership or authentic leadership. In fact, the starting point of good leadership is self-management, because when you have yourself under control you can pay attention to others, enhancing your social intelligence and your focus.

I had been thinking about the challenge of self-management over the years, and then my brilliant dressage coach, Niall Quirk, gave me a copy of *The Chimp Paradox*.

In the book, Dr Steven Peters offers a beautiful analysis of the mind and human nature using some of the latest research as well as simple metaphors to help us understand and manage what is happening inside our heads.

He begins by describing the different parts of the brain, with simple names we can all relate to. The first is the Human. That is you, the person supposedly in charge of things, and this is the executive function of the brain. Then there's the Computer, which does all of the automatic stuff you don't have to worry about, from keeping your body working to carrying out the actions that have become automated, like Roger Federer taking a great shot in tennis. The Computer processes at lightning speed, whereas the Human processes slowly and sequentially. The third part is what Peters calls the Chimp. The Chimp is your emotional brain, technically known as the limbic brain. The Chimp is the centre of your feelings and drives the actions that emanate from those feelings. Whereas the Human is rational and thoughtful, the Chimp is insecure, emotional and impulsive. These three parts of the brain can work together in harmony, but any of them can take charge and they can all get into conflict with one another. When that happens, the Chimp usually wins.

The Human and the Chimp often do battle and that is what's happening when people behave inconsistently. I've found this metaphor to be very powerful when competing on my horse because what I do is inherently scary. I don't know anyone who doesn't get bad stage fright before they ride a cross country course. Part of the thrill is overcoming that fear, but if you let it take over, mistakes can happen. Or, if you allow yourself to obsess too much about what you have to do, you can over-process, which gets in the way of the flow, again leading to mistakes. A bit of adrenalin and stage fright is a good thing; too much can be destructive.

Peters suggests that this stage fright is caused by the Chimp gradually taking over; the Chimp is irrational, emotional and tends towards catastrophic thinking, making you too scared to perform at your best. When I'm warming up at the start the Chimp is catastrophising: "What if he (the horse) forgets to jump? What if he runs away? What if I fall off? I could get hurt really badly! What if he falls? I could get trapped underneath him! Maybe I'll lose my way on the course, that would be so embarrassing."

When you understand that, you can make friends with your Chimp. You can say to her: "Listen, it's ok, we've got this. You go and relax, enjoy the ride and we'll celebrate when it's over." I now do that if I get too wound up before I ride cross country and I can feel calm descending over me. I think about something else and don't engage in what I have to do until I'm in the starting box. There's nothing I can think about in the 20 minutes preceding that moment that will mean I have a better ride, so I box up the Chimp nicely and deliberately think about something else. When we jump out of that start box all my focus comes into play, years of training kick in, and if all goes well the ride will be the most thrilling, enjoyable five to eight minutes imaginable.

When someone loses control in a work discussion and behaves badly, one way to avoid getting into conflict with them is to remind yourself that you are not actually talking to them, but to their Chimp. That means you need to let the Chimp settle down before you try to have a rational discussion. Whatever you do, don't let your own Chimp get involved! The more you observe how your mind is operating and whether your decisions and actions are motivated by your Human or your Chimp, the more you will gain control over situations and be able to apply the ideas in this book. It takes work though, because the Chimp is strong – much stronger than the Human. Here is an example that Peters uses in the book, told in my own words.

You go for coffee with a friend and she offers you a delicious piece of cake with your coffee. You're dieting and this diet is really important to you. Unfortunately, it also means you're quite hungry. Your Chimp sees the cake and immediately says "Great, cake!" "No!" the Human replies, "I'm on a diet". (Of course this conversation is going on in your head; you haven't yet answered your friend, who is still waiting for a reply.) "But I'm hungry", says the Chimp, "and that cake looks delicious. Anyway, how can that one little piece of cake spoil anything, I've been good for ages. I deserve a reward!"

What do you think the Human is going to do? Most of us will have the cake, or at least I know I would. Peters goes on to give a lot of sound advice about managing your Chimp and becoming a better and happier person as a result.

Since it came out, *The Chimp Paradox* has been the most sold self-help book in the UK and I highly recommend it as a companion to this one, because if you really want to do something extraordinary, to achieve a really cheeky 10X target, you'll need to develop your self-management, which means you'll need to understand how your mind works and then put it to the best possible use. Extraordinary people, like the Schwarzeneggers or the Dalios of this world, seem to figure a lot of this out for themselves. The rest of us can benefit from taking ideas and advice from credible sources.

Part Three – The 5-Step Process

"Life punishes the vague wish and rewards the specific ask."

Tim Ferriss

Chapter 14

Setting objectives

❦

Before we get onto the 5-Step process, let's think for a moment about how you might want to tackle setting your objectives. The approach that I usually recommend for clients is to start with SMART (Specific, Measurable, Achievable, Realistic and Timed) objectives and then make a plan to achieve them. Setting SMART objectives really does work because you can easily track how you are doing against them and record those small wins that keep you motivated.

There's another approach that might also be worth considering.

From reading authors like Grant Cordone and Dr Bob Rotella, I think it might sometimes be worth going for the biggest objectives you can imagine in important areas of your life. In an early eBook that I read on the topic of sports psychology, by Australian eventer Peter Haynes, he described how he aimed for what seemed an impossible dream – becoming the Australian Eventing Champion.

Much to his surprise he did become the Australian Champion and afterwards he wished he'd had even bigger dreams, like riding in the Australian team at the Olympics, or even winning an Olympic gold medal.

Dr Rotella makes the point that people rarely exceed their dreams. Tiger Woods wanted to beat Jack Nicklaus's record of winning 18 golfing Masters. He was stuck at 14 for a long time. You could see that as failing to achieve your dreams or you could also describe Tiger Woods as the second-best golfer in the history of the game, so far. Now that he's winning again, he could still achieve that extravagant objective: to be the best.

Cordone's suggestion is that we aim for crazy goals, keep them in front of us all the time, and then put massive amounts of effort, what he calls 10X, into achieving them. This approach is counterintuitive in some ways. If you want to feel like a winner, you might not want to set crazy objectives that you are not likely to achieve. Then again, if you want to go beyond what you even think is possible, why not try?

This year I'm going to play with a different idea. I'm taking two of my most important objectives and expanding them significantly. My 10X might not be Cordone's but I'm prepared to put everything I've got into these two goals. And the older I get the more ambitious I get, because my time is more limited.

When I turned 50 I told myself that I wanted the next 25 years to matter as much as the past 25, if not more.

I make that point in terms of goal setting because I'm currently driven by this timing, and, by drawing confidence from the fact that I've reached my half century as fit, healthy and ambitious as ever. Your life will be in a different place, so choose what works best for you. Some years we need to be realistic about what we can accomplish. Any working mother with small children that I know is way too busy to set crazy objectives. She is already doing exceptionally well to be holding down a job, rearing children and trying to have some kind of personal life, so the 10X goals can probably wait a bit.

Instead, what she might need is time for regular, weekly exercise, so she can build fitness and have some time to herself.

I firmly believe that you can have everything in a lifetime – well, maybe not everything, but an awful lot – just not all at the same time.

Choose your moment to set 10X goals.

One of the main benefits you'll get from sitting down quietly for an hour and going through this process is that you'll have a chance to reflect on what is important to you and to develop a plan to achieve it.

Just because you want something doesn't automatically mean you will get it. If your dreams are ambitious, are you really prepared for the work and sacrifices it will take to achieve them?

Running a marathon sounds great. Getting up at 4am on a winter's morning to put the miles in before work is a lot less fun. One thing is certain though – if you don't aim to run that marathon and if you don't put the plan in place, you'll never do it. And you may surprise yourself. Once you get into the habit of training, when that winter morning comes, it will be much harder for anything to stop you getting up and out there.

Life is full of the unexpected and sometimes it can get between you and your dreams. For example, I compete seriously in my sport and for that I need my horse to be fit and capable. If he gets injured, we are not going to achieve our objectives for the year and there's nothing I can do about it.

Similarly, if your dream was to get the promotion you've always wanted but the business goes through a serious downturn and you get retrenched, that is most likely going to be a horrible experience and it will also mean the end of that particular dream, for now.

In *The 7 Habits of Highly Effective People,* Stephen Covey talked about the Sphere of Control and the Sphere of Influence. When your dreams and objectives involve other people, be aware that they may not work out as you hope. Humbling though it can be, you are not responsible for the actions of others. Or, to put it another way, there will be people within your sphere of influence who are not within your sphere of control.

After we published the first edition of this book, under the title *That Further Shore*, many readers, including some of my own friends, told me that they used the 5-Steps to think more deeply about improving relationships with others: husbands, wives, children, friends, partners and business colleagues. If you have relationships in your life that are not working, this can be one of the richest and most rewarding areas to focus on, and it is a wonderful place to invest your time and energy. Science tells us that our relationship with our community, with others, is the richest source of happiness available to us. Some of the feedback I have had from readers who have turned relationships around completely has been deeply touching.

I know from personal experience that it does not always work, particularly if the person you care about is suffering from the terrible diseases of depression or addiction, or both. As Poorna Bell describes heartachingly in *Chase the Rainbow*, the very nature of these misunderstood diseases means that it does not matter what you do, the other person simply cannot respond in an appropriate way and your influence is almost nil. Anyone who has dealt with severe depression or addiction will understand instantly what I am describing.

If you are in that situation, remember that you cannot be held responsible for outcomes that involve another person. You can manage your own behaviour, you can set objectives around how you handle yourself, and choose your response to the situations in which you find yourself. In doing that, you can grow in strength and self-respect. But, if the situation involves other people, be aware, you might not get the desired outcome. Even more importantly, it's worth remembering that the outcome you wanted might never have been an option in the first place, because it was not in your control.

That doesn't have to be a disaster, but it does mean we have to be flexible and, at times, prepared to adjust our hopes and our expectations of life.

Alta's Story

I met Alta in February 2016 when we started the MPhil programme at Stellenbosch University Business School. Alta was looking forward to 2016. She worked in a senior HR role in a big company and to help her career she signed up for a course in Executive Coaching. Doing this programme was her dream.

Alta started the course in February, enthused and excited about the year ahead. At the start of the second module in March, she was a different person. She'd just been retrenched after 22 years of working for the same company. She was completely shocked; her friends wondered if she would get over it.

To everyone's surprise, she did, and faster than expected. She always had a passion for the environment and wanted to do something that would have a positive impact. She got together with a colleague who had also been retrenched and they identified a range of products aimed at helping the environment and started importing them.

The business is doing well, and Alta is having the most fun she's ever had in her life. She's been through some personal ups and downs, but she loves the business, and the challenges it brings, as well as the positive impact it's having on the environment.

Some of the products are specifically aimed at water saving, and as Cape Town faced a severe drought, Alta and her colleagues were proud of the contribution they were making. Change is painful, but it often leads to positive outcomes; it certainly did for Alta. In December 2017, she was one of a small cohort who graduated from the programme in the shortest possible time, another achievement of which to be proud.

The 5-Step Process

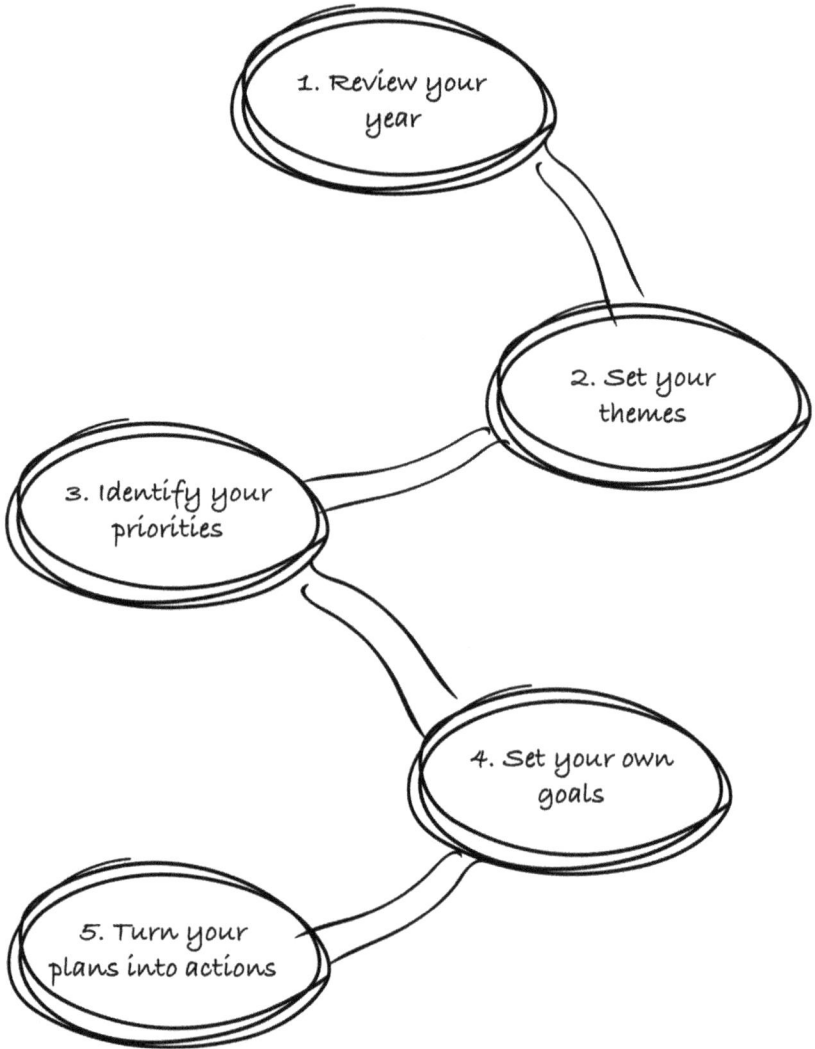

1. Review your year

2. Set your themes

3. Identify your priorities

4. Set your own goals

5. Turn your plans into actions

Planning can change your life

❧

The 5-Step Process

Setting the right number of SMART (Specific, Measurable, Achievable, Realistic and Timed) objectives and putting a schedule in place to achieve them really does work. If you want to throw in a couple of really big multipliers and see if that helps to stretch you, then try it. I'm doing it this year, but only on two of my objectives. All the rest are SMART.

There are a lot of great books and theories out there to help you achieve your goals. What's different about this one? This approach is not just about helping you to achieve your goals; it's about getting your focus right so that your goals align with your values, and with what really matters to you. Sometimes you might be surprised by what you find out about yourself.

I sat down in January to plan my year, as I have done every year since I discovered the 5-Step approach.

When I did Step 3 of the 5-Steps, which is where you choose your themes for the year, I thought about my whole life. Normally I prioritise my work and my competitive sport and set ambitious goals in both areas. Two years ago achieving my study goals was also important and I was pleased that I had completed the MPhil programme in the minimum possible time. Thinking about this year's themes, work had to be at the top of the list as we've set some pretty demanding targets for the business in a tough economic environment. This book was second on the list. I thought that getting it published would be really hard, but then I met Wilhelm Crous, my publisher, who said his company, KR Publishing, would like to publish and promote it.

The first edition was published in 2018, and in 2019 I proposed a new book to Wilhelm. He loves the concept but asked for a revision and a relaunch of this one first, because he believed it could target a bigger audience. That meant my priority shifted to getting the new edition ready for publication.

The third theme was obviously my riding objectives. Or was it? As I sat and brainstormed I realised that setting ambitious riding objectives this year would just put pressure on me and take my focus off what really matters. I'm now at a level where I can comfortably compete at a notch below my ultimate target and not worry about it too much. We had some good results in 2018 and even won some events. So I decided to stay with my two main themes and even to think about the possibility of selling my horse and taking a break from the sport of eventing, if that's what it takes to achieve the multiplier goal in my business.

Whoever you are, think about the importance of prioritising what really matters as you set your themes for the year. If your kids are growing up fast and you're not spending enough time with them, prioritise that. If you need to address health issues, put that at the top. If you need to sit down and think about your finances, good, this is the time to figure that out. Maybe its planning your dream holiday. Fine, even if it takes more than a year to save enough, commit to it now.

If you're at the stage of your life where you want to focus on your business and career themes and go big on those, great, do it! But still take the time to think of your whole life and make sure you're not missing something deeply important, even if it may seem more day-to-day, or pedestrian.

Step 1 prepares the ground for Steps 2 and 3. These are often the most challenging and rewarding steps in the whole process. Step 2 is where you choose your focus. This sets the stage for everything else that happens to you this year, so enjoy the process and engage in it with all your heart.

It does not take too long to do, but make sure you take enough time to think about yourself holistically. Take account of every aspect of your life: work, home, finances, family, sport, health, fitness and anything else that is important.

All you need is a pen, a notepad, a cup of coffee and a quiet hour to yourself.

Ready to begin?

Step 1 – Review the past year

1. Review your
year

Take a notepad and write down what you've achieved in the year. Think about things like:

- ambitions, achieved or not;
- creative work;
- new skills you've developed or new behaviours you have learned;
- work successes;
- your network: people you met or got to know better;
- places you visited;
- things you achieved at home;
- your health; and
- family highlights.

Now write down any disappointments. Things like:

- setbacks at work;
- health issues you've had to deal with;
- moments where you had to change plans or faced difficulties;
- blocks or hurdles to achieving what you want;
- financial or practical challenges; and
- difficult family or friend situations.

If you did this exercise last year, now is the time to look back at last year's plan. Compare what you aimed to achieve with your actual achievements.

Next, write a headline for the last 12 months.

If you were being interviewed and were asked to describe the year, what would you say? Don't be too hard on yourself – sometimes it's the journey that's important, not always the goals.

Step 1 – My review of 2018

To help you, here is my review of 2018. I've taken out some of the more personal themes but this gives you an idea of what you should be thinking about. Re-reading it as I include it here, I can see I'm quite tough on myself. That's ok, it's who I am. The language of this is quite informal and so should yours be; this is your own document and is not really meant to be shared.

As I looked back at my objectives for 2018 I had to smile. Apart from making this book an out and out bestseller, which was a 10x goal that we continue to work on, I've achieved what I set out to do. Outcomes that seemed impossible at the beginning of the year unfurled and became reality as the year progressed.

In January I had no business and no book. Now I am a published author, whose readers write to me and tell me how my book has changed their lives. The work of promoting the book has given me experience on TV and radio and I've really enjoyed that journey and learned some important lessons along the way. For example: you have to look good on TV. How ridiculously obvious is that? Looking good on TV takes different colours and much more make-up and hair-styling than normal life. Coming across naturally in a TV studio is also a learning curve, and in my last two interviews I felt I was getting there. (Check out our website (www. woodburnmannlsi.co.za) or my LinkedIn profile (linkedin.com/in/ sarah-arnot-39546a) to see these interviews.)

Finding a publisher happened surprisingly quickly and once he committed I immediately sat down and expanded the book. It feels like the writing got better and better and we've already agreed my next book will be about leadership, although from a completely different angle, and I'm really looking forward to working on it.

The business has been fantastic. We did hit our financial objective despite a tough economic environment toward late 2018. We also put some solid client development in place. I spent much of the year capturing my approach to leadership and creating a framework that we call The Leadership Sphere. When we presented it to a few key potential clients in November they loved it. The concept is original and fresh and all of our leadership services fit into the Leadership Sphere. That work has been the basis of our continued growth in 2019.

Best of all I couldn't have chosen a better partner than Andrew Woodburn. He is a much more experienced entrepreneur than I am and I learn from him constantly. At the same time I have found I am better at developing business than I thought I would be, and indeed really enjoy it. Andrew, like our clients, believes I have something fresh to bring to leadership at the top level and that belief is a great support. Building business in a tough economy has not been easy, yet it proves we have a concept that clients want even in these times. As and when the economy turns we will be ready to grow.

The continued pressure of travel and work has been tough on my work-life balance. I cut back completely on competitions in 2018, although I did have one fantastic and unexpected win and a few runner-up prizes in eventing. I also did something I'd said I wouldn't and upgraded to the next level, CNC*, the level where you start competing at international heights and standards. I made the mistake of doing it at a championship where the cross country track was huge, my horse was overwhelmed and I ended up falling off. I learned another lesson though, which is that I cannot have my head in two big games at once. If I am putting all my energy and passion into building this business, I can't put the work needed into competing at a higher level, however much I might want to. The result was that I am taking a step back and may even stop riding for a while to focus on work and the rest of my work-life balance.

Simplifying my life in order to put my focus where it needs to be will be an overarching theme for 2019.

Despite completing my MPhil in 2017 I didn't feel a great sense of accomplishment; 2018 was completely different: it was an extraordinary year and I believe it has set the stage for great years to come.

As part of the 5-Step process , I write an annual headline. For 2018 it looked like this. Leadership expert publishes first book and founds exciting new company with a profound purpose: to bring the science of leadership to the boardrooms of Africa.

Step 2 – Set your themes for this year

2. Set your themes

Steps 2 and 3 are the really fun part of this entire process. Step 2 delivers the most important outcome – where you should focus your efforts. Even if you don't see yourself as a creative person, you'll find this part invigorating and even creative. That's because it's intrinsically about YOU.

You are setting themes first: general areas of life where you want to focus your attention and, this is important, bring about change.

We're not looking at specifics here: use your reflections on the past year to help you set your themes for the next 12 months.

Write down the three areas of your life you want to focus on this year.

Not more than three. If you achieve them early you can add more, but for now focus on just three themes.

Here are some suggestions to kick start your thinking process:

work; business; money; leadership; skills development; work/life balance; time-management; productivity; fitness and health; family and friends; fun; travel and exploration; home; love and relationships; giving back.

Step 2 – example

For my three themes in 2019 I chose:

- building the new business with ambitious targets;
- finishing the new edition of my first book and completing the next one; and
- simplifying my life.

Step 3 – Identify your priorities

3. Identify your priorities

Now you're going to brainstorm by inducing a state of "flow" that should allow you to become more creative and move you to a deeper state of thinking about your themes. This might sound unlikely, but concentrating really hard on one thing for five minutes brings about a creative, reflective state of mind that should lead to interesting new connections and ideas.

Take a piece of paper and a pen. Write down your first theme and for at least five minutes (set the timer on your phone) jot down ideas about how your life could be better a year from today. Concentrate on outcomes – the best possible outcomes you can imagine. This is the time to dream and I call these "dream sheets".

Keep the pen moving, draw as well as write, get it all down. Don't lift the pen from the page for the whole five minutes.

I use Evernote as my online notebook, though I also have a paper notebook I bring to meetings. For this exercise, I use pen and an old fashioned A4 pad. When I did this last year I lost my paper sheets, so this time I photographed them when I was finished and added them to Evernote. That way I now have everything together when I come to review the year.

As you do this exercise remember to be ambitious; put no limits on what you could achieve.

Build on your ideas. If you want to be creative, what does it look like? A book, a painting course or finding a way to take your team to a new level of delivery?

Keep less glamorous objectives in mind; maybe you need to address some aspect of your health or well-being?

Try to be specific – it's not "get fit", it's run 15km a week or walk the Otter Trail. Think about outcomes – the best outcomes you can imagine. Thinking about outcomes is the clever thing about this exercise, because it helps to crystallise what you really want and gets it into words. Be bold and brave at this point. You can refine it later; for now, dream big.

Now do the same for the next two themes.

You should find this process exciting and invigorating and it might be that one of the priorities starts to take precedence. That is good news because it means the exercise is helping you to prioritise better.

Ideas might emerge that surprise you. This exercise can be a way of tapping into your subconscious; of pulling out the ideas you've had over the last year but forgotten as other more urgent thoughts take over. Do not reject any surprising thoughts – they may be the important ones.

Some people have dreams that appear huge and aspirational: write a book; earn a million Rands; raise a million Dollars; start a PhD. Other people's dreams might not appear so demanding: lose weight; get fit; learn to cook really well; take a dream vacation. Does it matter? Of course not. These are your dreams. If you've always wanted to be a better cook, then that is your dream. Succeeding might lead to expanding your dream or to many happy, confident hours in the kitchen. Do not allow other people to influence your dream — decide for yourself.

When you've done all three, take a short break.

Deliver the book to clients and friends as an ebook with beautiful design by the end of January. Ask M who her friend is who can help me with illustrations and design. I won't have time to do that part myself, learning the tools takes too long. Going to be a big cost.

Use that to find a publisher to publish it by the end of 2018. How do I do that? Ideas that come to mind right now are find an agent - look online there must be some. Who in SA publishes business books? Who published Salome's book? Make it a bestseller - well that's kind of a joke as it's unlikely but at least research the elements that go into a good book and keep doing that. Even if I find a publisher keep working at that because they will never care as much as I do.

Marketing ideas well if I get it published I need to figure out the best way to market it and make sure it gets attention. My own social networks, and asking friends to help with the amazon part. And book launches. And promoting it - maybe M can help with this need to see what she would charge

Design - need to keep thinking about design and keep on thinking about what works in design very important.

Book launches, could have some fun with that, see if we can get lots of friends to come

Find an agent who loves my work? How to go about doing that, need to flesh out that idea. Start writing the next book be proactive. Talk to people I know who have published but I don't know if they are willing to share contacts, can but try. Wiley is an obvious one, but UK based and my stories are so SA? Also KR - see they publish people who's books I've read.

Having a book will be great for speaking gigs and to share with clients going forward. Really cool, this is something I want to do.

Figure 8: Example of a dream sheet

This is my own dream sheet from January 2018. The theme was "finish my eBook and find a publisher". The amazing thing about this theme was that it fell quickly into place. In the first two weeks of January I worked on getting an eBook out for my friends and clients, then a new acquaintance introduced me to Wilhelm Crous, the owner of KR Publishing. They like books that are ready to go, so they gave me some feedback and offered to publish almost immediately. I went to work straightaway to incorporate their feedback and develop some more material in places. Once I had got that far, I returned to my themes and started thinking, "What next? How do I use this published book to support my other objectives?"

I'm using a personal example but there's a powerful message here. The minute you write something down as a goal, you start moving towards it. In a Californian study, Dr Gail Matthews looked at a varied group of professionals and divided them up simply by whether they wrote down their goals. Astonishingly, those who wrote down their goals were 42% more likely to achieve them. I've seen how true this is. I've always wanted to publish a book, but this is the first time in my life that I've specifically written down: "Get my book published" as a goal. If I had not made that written commitment, I probably would not have mentioned my book to Debbie Goodman of Jackhammer in Cape Town. She immediately, and very kindly, introduced me to my publisher.

I cannot stress this enough: when you write something down and commit to it, you have already started to make it come true. Why? Because your attention zeroes in on it without you even realising. You start to focus, explicitly, on what you want. That is why it's so important to spend time on Steps 2 and 3 choosing the right themes for your year and brainstorming the outcomes you want and what they look like. Once you circle those and create your objectives around them in Step 4, you are well on the road to successfully achieving them. This sounds extraordinary, but it's true.

Before we move on let me share one of my favourite stories with you. There's a gnarly old US equestrian star called Denny Emerson. He has continued to ride well into his 70s, and he has written a wonderful book: *How Good Riders Get Good*. In it he tells the story of the flea jar, which, in my own words, goes like this:

If you get a large jar and put some fleas in it, the fleas will try to jump out of the jar. If the jar has a lid on it, the fleas will bang their little heads against the lid and they obviously will not be able to escape from the jar. After a while they still jump, but they don't jump high enough to bang their heads, because they've learned that they cannot get out of the jar. Now here is the thing. If you then take the lid off the jar, the fleas will never jump out; they have learned their lesson.

Too often we can be like that. We think we are confined and we don't reach too high for fear of banging our heads. We limit our choices. When I first raised the topic of choices in Chapter 3, I described how we narrow our frames and limit ourselves to binary options when so many more might be available. Broadening our frames and being really creative about our options is like building ourselves a bigger jar.

I often tell this story when I give motivational speeches about leadership and transformational change. The topic sounds simple, but it's really about helping people understand that they have far more power than they realise to change their lives; if they want to, that is. The story of the flea jar is a powerful illustration of how we become trapped by our day-to-day lives and it's the story people talk about when they see me again. They will say: "I've got a bigger jar."

Step 4 – Set your goals for the year

4. Set your own goals

After the break, return to your "dream sheets" and circle the ideas and objectives that jump out at you, or seem the most important, or both. You want to feel inspired and excited and you want these things to have a positive impact on your life.

Now write them down as a list.

Aim for about three objectives per theme – a maximum of nine. If it's a big one – like earning an important new qualification – you can focus on just that area. You should end up with three to nine objectives.

Now start to break those objectives down into tasks or create a schedule that will start you on the road to achieving them.

Maybe it's just me, but I find this bit quite hard. This is where you turn your themes into objectives and then a real plan. I tend to overload my life and, perhaps because I do many different things, switching quickly between them can be a challenge.

What are those parts?

1. Homemaker, stepmother, step-granny, daughter and sister (family is always the most important to me).

2. Coach to senior executives, specifically public company CEOs.
3. Partner in a fast-growing leadership services business.
4. Social life – time for friends and family.
5. Competitive rider.
6. Running a thriving Airbnb business.

Though they might take up time, some of these don't belong on my list of themes. Take the Airbnb business; I've run it for a couple of years now. The advantage of the platform is that it handles the bookings and the money. It also reminds you when guests are arriving, so there's no risk of forgetting a booking. It's an efficient process now that fits seamlessly into day to day household management. I might want to grow it at some point, but it doesn't need to be a priority this year. The guesthouse consistently gets five-star reviews, bookings grow despite the competition and, with some help from those around me, we are listed as Superhosts, proving how well the process works. That aspect of farm life doesn't need more attention this year.

> Some of your objectives will need you to change your habits, so make sure you don't try to achieve too much at once.

For example, if you want to exercise regularly, set a schedule you can live with and stick to it. If you cannot stick with it, make it easier or try a different form of exercise – one that appeals to you more – and keep trying until you can stick to it.

If you want to write a book or complete a thesis, commit to a writing programme that works for you. It might only be a paragraph before you go to bed, but make sure you commit and stick to the process you choose.

I have a busy life and I can find this exercise of setting my objectives overwhelming. If you find yourself in the same situation, here is what I've learned over the years. Forcing yourself to focus on your priorities – the things that you really want to achieve – can help you to declutter the rest of your life or deprioritise some things until your top priority hits target.

This reluctance to focus objectives is especially true when I do this exercise with teams. They come up with such great ideas and outcomes in Step 3 that they don't want to refine them down to just three themes and three objectives in Step 4. Yet if they don't, the focus dissipates and they struggle to achieve anything at all.

I've learned that it's better to ask them to choose one or two themes that need a long-term focus in order to be successful, and then one or two themes where they believe they can deliver quickly. If they deliver, they can bring in a new theme. If they don't, they need to go back and understand the roadblocks and see if they can solve them or find a workaround.

Here is an example of how I prioritised one of my themes when a big roadblock appeared, and how I managed to stay focussed.

In 2017, my most important objective was to complete my studies and graduate by the end of the year. We were warned that this would be a huge challenge, and that most candidates don't finish their theses in time to graduate within the minimum two years.

By August I realised that I needed a lot of research hours if I was going to be finished by the end of September. At the same time, a lucrative work project arrived. I felt completely overwhelmed. I sat down and looked at my objectives, then I saw the solution. I simply deprioritised my sport. I did not stop, but I accepted that I was not going to hit my sporting objectives for the year.

The impact of this was extraordinarily liberating, and having reprioritised, I nailed my most important objectives by the end of the year.

That is the beauty of this process; it doesn't just help you set your objectives at the start of the year, it also helps you to prioritise what is most important as the months go by. If you start feeling overwhelmed, you can use it to figure out what is most important and narrow down your focus. Conversely, if things are swinging along nicely, you can increase your scope and push yourself to achieve more.

Here are my objectives for 2018 for two of my themes: the business and the books.

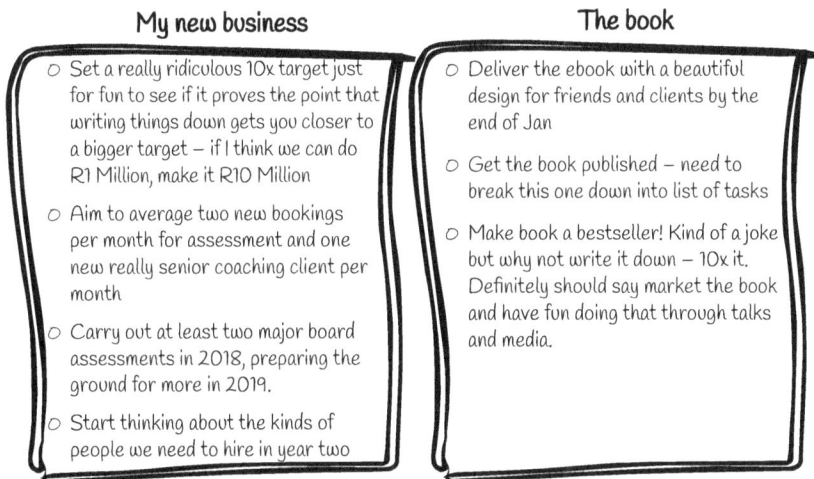

My new business

○ Set a really ridiculous 10x target just for fun to see if it proves the point that writing things down gets you closer to a bigger target – if I think we can do R1 Million, make it R10 Million

○ Aim to average two new bookings per month for assessment and one new really senior coaching client per month

○ Carry out at least two major board assessments in 2018, preparing the ground for more in 2019.

○ Start thinking about the kinds of people we need to hire in year two

The book

○ Deliver the ebook with a beautiful design for friends and clients by the end of Jan

○ Get the book published – need to break this one down into list of tasks

○ Make book a bestseller! Kind of a joke but why not write it down – 10x it. Definitely should say market the book and have fun doing that through talks and media.

Figure 9: Sarah's objectives

Apps that can help you

I find mobile apps useful to help me achieve my objectives.

1. **Hey Jude**: I first learned about virtual assistants from Tim Ferriss in *The Four-Hour Week*, but I couldn't figure out the best way to use them. Last year a friend told me about Hey Jude, which is a virtual assistant that helps with all those smaller, more urgent tasks that need to be done today – things that would often go on your 'To Do' list, like remembering to send a present to someone, to make a restaurant reservation or to book a doctor's appointment. Or realising as you are on

the way to the airport that you need to book a car because originally you thought you would use Uber, but actually a car would be better (this happens to me a lot as I commute between the Cape and Johannesburg).

Send Jude a message and Jude will take care of it.

2. **Audible**: It took me a while to get into audio books, then I realised they are great company on long drives – and South Africa is a large country. They are good company out running too, or even on holiday when you want to read, but you also want to look at the place. Above all, audio books allowed me to increase the number of books I read, which is great as I'm constantly on a quest for new information. I like business books and autobiographies. Recently I listened to the audio-autobiographies of both Richard Branson and Arnold Schwarzenegger. Curiously enough, though I enjoyed Branson's book, I could relate to Schwarzenegger's more and I found it much more inspiring. I've shared some insights from Schwarzenegger, and how Tim Ferriss piqued my interest in him, earlier in this book.

3. **Pomodoro**: This is a straightforward but very useful timer. Science suggests that short breaks refresh us and improve the quality of our output. What is clever about Pomodoro is that it gives you 25-minute blocks of time, then suggests you take a 5-minute break. After two hours, it suggests a longer break. When you are trying to focus on big tasks like writing reports, this is helpful. I also find it keeps me honest about how I spend my time. It's easy to sit at my desk for five hours and think I've done five hours of productive work, but as I only set the Pomodoro clock when I get really stuck into the task, I might find I've only done five or six 25-minute chunks of time.

4. **Evernote:** A really handy Notebook app that sits on your laptop as well as your devices. I use the free version and find it more than adequate for my needs. It's handy because

it syncs to all your devices, you can drag and drop emails and photos, even email attachments, and you can set up a Notebook for every project. The search function is terrific – if you can't remember which Notebook you wrote something in, you just search for it. Notebooks are also projects that can be shared with others, so it can be useful for teamwork. As I said above, I do like to use pen and paper and I sometimes photograph the page and drop it into the Evernote Notebook. I try lots of apps and then abandon them, but Evernote has stuck.

5. **Running apps**: I try to run three times a week, and it's quite easy to think I achieved that when I really did not. Now I use an app called Wahoo Fitness to record my runs. Lots of people prefer Strava, which links to multiple devices, watches and heart monitors. These apps work in similar ways – they measure your routes, heart rate and speed, which is enough for me, though they can do much more, especially if you like to share your progress with your friends. In my case, the front page gives me my running history for the last four weeks, so it keeps me honest.

6. **The 7-minute workout:** South African's refer to going on safari as "going to the bush". I love the bush; the solace of nature, the rhythm of the days, bumbling around in 4-wheel drive safari vehicles at dawn to find the wildlife of Africa and share special moments with these animals in their natural habitat. Sharing sundowners with friends at sunset on a koppie (a small hill) with a breathtaking view. Hearing the echo of jackals or hyenas howling, or the grunt of the hunting lion. I am not a great photographer, I just like to share the animals' space and learn about their habits. Although not a "birder" I also enjoy learning about and watching the myriad of birds that thrive in Southern Africa. I like to acquire knowledge and my grandmothers taught me to love plants and trees, so I learn the names of the trees and flowers in the different habitats that we visit.

As a driven, busy person I used to become impatient as I watched animals and waited for the next thing to happen. Now I draw a lesson from meditation and tell myself "animal time". Animals have no meeting schedule, they are not driven by objectives (other than finding food, water and shelter). They simply live in the moment. Moving into animal time is part of the restorative dimension of being in the bush.

What I don't like so much is that you can't go running if you are in a proper reserve like the Kruger Park. The Big Five, elephant, buffalo, rhinoceros, lion and leopard are everywhere: it's just not safe.

A couple of years ago I read the research on high intensity workouts and why they might be just as effective as longer low intensity workouts. There are several high intensity apps available and I like the original Johnson and Johnson 7 Minute Workout; there are many others. I tend not to use it regularly as I prefer a combination of running and Pilates as a general fitness regime, but when I'm in a place where it's problematic to run, for any reason, the 7 Minute Workout is ideal. All you need is a small space and a chair or bench. It works so well that I often come back from my break fitter than when I arrived.

7. **Airbnb**: I joined Airbnb a few years ago. There are two cottages on the farm that were decorated for a big family wedding and not used much, so I thought I would give it a try and it's been a great success. I love the platform because it takes care of the reservation, the money, and reminds you when guests are coming to stay. The place gets consistent 5* reviews and has Superhost status. At a time when I was working less because I was studying, it was a welcome source of revenue. The guests are lovely – the kind of person who books a farm stay through Airbnb generally fits in well here. I mention Airbnb specifically in case you find yourself in a situation where you

need to generate more income quickly and have suitable accommodation that you are not using.

Now, let's turn those plans into actions...

Step 5 – Turn your plans into actions

5. Turn your plans into actions

Take a calendar and mark up the commitments you already have in place.

Choose one objective from your list. Now write down what you must do in January, February and March (the first quarter of the year) to achieve that goal by the end of March.

If it will take longer, spread your actions throughout the year but make a detailed first quarter plan.

Now start breaking up the themes into objectives and ideas and put them into buckets, like Colette did in Chapter 1. That will make it easier to think about the actions and processes needed to achieve those goals. Here's an example from my plan to start my own new business. I didn't really know how it was going to work, so I put everything I could think of into buckets and when I wasn't sure what to do next, I referred back to those and found something I could move forward with. Not everything worked out exactly as I imagined it would, but when I look back at this list, the business grew in every dimension I had identified.

MY NEW BUSINESS

Building business

Aim for two new assessment clients per month
One big new coaching client per month
Keep pushing to 1 big board assessment
Understand and push for the WBM LS pieces so I can start delivering those

Revenues

Track the numbers and make sure I am building against the 10x target
That's going to mean constant month on month growth

Marketing

Start networking with previous clients
Use the book to get my name out more? That could also be a PR campaign
Consider a launch party for the business when we've nailed a few clients
Consider a thought piece, maybe on ethical leadership

Create materials

Develop new services
Develop more case studies
Develop beautiful marketing materials, website, etc
Develop great client deliverables, work with Jacques to improve the dashboard
ID more learning sources for myself

Internal marketing

This is really important – the search consultants need to know this is easy to sell, great added value for their clients and fantastic for their own bottom line
Invest time in getting to know the people

CLIENTS

If the business grows fast think about the people side and the kinds of people we need to bring on board to help us. Need someone who can do great presentation development? A project manager and a new consultant?

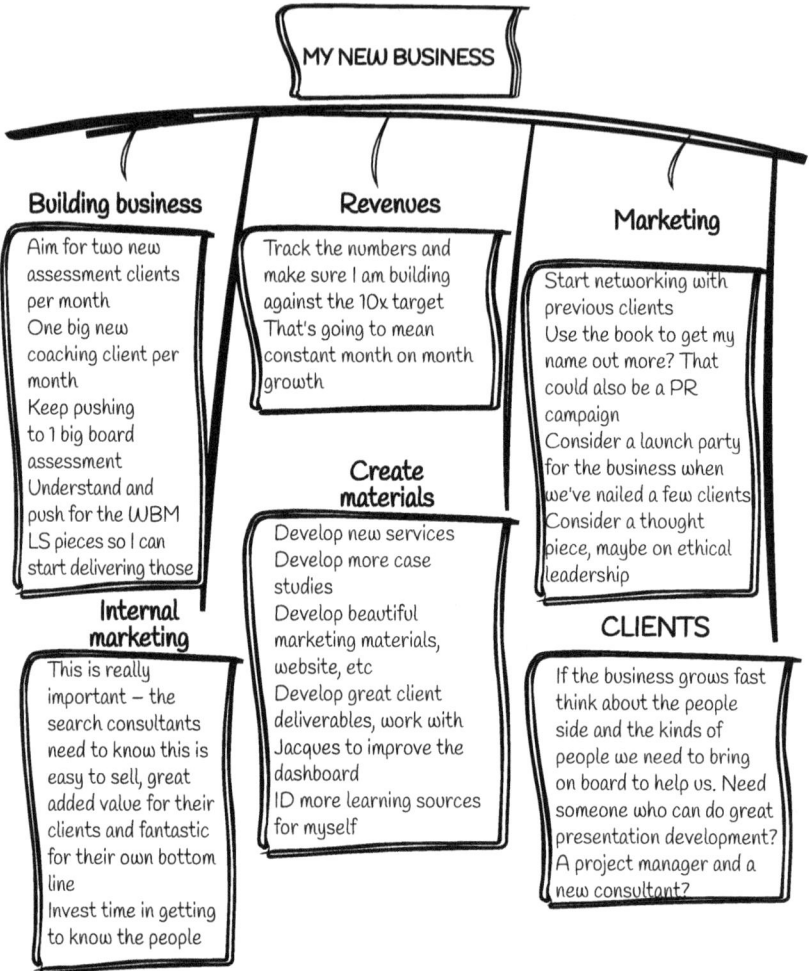

Figure 10: Breaking actions down and sorting them into buckets

The next thing to do is to create a simple one-page chart for the year. I've put my 2019 objectives in here. When you do this, you can have a whole page for each month if you want. What you'll see is that you'll have quite a clear idea of what to do for the first few months, and then it gets a bit vaguer. That's fine, as long as you go back and flesh out the later months as they draw nearer. That can be very motivating because you'll see how many "small wins" you have achieved. On this page I've included commitments that are in already in place, like travel and competitions, so I can clearly see how easily they fit into my planning, or if they actually just get in the way. This helps you to focus and prioritise. Here is how mine looks.

January
- Aim for a calm first two weeks and head to Joburg week three
- Start getting marketing meetings in the diary
- Plan next Marketing Date
- Follow up on leads from 2018
- Write to publisher about new book idea
- Decide if going to sell Filipe (my horse)

February
- Eventing in Noordhoek
- Aim for 8 marketing meetings and at least four proposals into market
- Keep working on big project proposal 2x new clients

March
- Follow through with plan to sell Filipe
- Continue with marketing – 6 x meetings and 4 x proposals minimum in March
- Book one big project
- ID possible new hires – 1x admin, 1x consultant
- Confirm new book with publisher

April
- Easter this month – make sure to take advantage of the break
- If plan is to book 50 units, by now should have booked 15
- Eventing in Noordhoek

May
- If selling horse by now he needs to jump big tracks
- Focus on delivery of client work
- Where are we on more resources?
- Marketing next steps
- New book on track?
- Eventing in Sandringham?

June
- Selling horse on track – aim is to sell by July / August
- Next big piece of client work is where?
- New resources on board
- Plans for growth of business?
- Date for publication of book

July
- Plan marketing launch for September – maybe using new book
- Focus on units in – what do we have to do to hit our numbers by end of year?
- Plan for new resources, are they in? contributing, does that help us to grow?
- New Service offerings?
- Horse sale should be on track

August
- New marketing day should be designed and planned, maybe two before end of year.
- Another big project in pipeline?
- ID more team coaching and CEO coaching opportuties. Book 1 or 2 more CEOs for coaching, need to grow this
- New services offerings in development? In market

September
- Start thinking about how AW could grow the finalist candidate assessment piece.
- Check in on numbers – where do we stand?
- By now horse should be sold and book should be launched. Big book launch? Travel US/UK/Ireland/France

October
- Ensure that we have work to end of year
- Start planning into 2020 where is the work coming from? Can we have client projects booked into January so we don't have a quiet start?
- Coaching clients?
- New services – based on book? Can that be done. T up marketing for 2020 around book and services

November
- Step back and look at value chain as we plan 2020. What's worked what hasn't.
- Book new work in November to take us through to Feb 2020 Economy, growth?
- Plan ahead to marketing meetings in 2020.
- Get creative about how to push growth.

December
- Make sure we have everything cleared up and ready by December 15 latest.
- Plan 2020 in place so we hit ground fast in January.
- Are we looking to 10x growth again?
- Resource allocation, have we got it right or is this something we still need to do?

Figure 11: Planning the year

Write down your objectives, print them out and keep them on your desk. I've laminated mine. The buckets and the year plan are also near to hand, because they tell me *how* I'm going to achieve my objectives. At some point I might use a SWOT analysis as described in Chapter 1, or some of the tools mentioned in Part Two.

Keep a date with yourself at the start of every month to check on your progress. If something isn't working, it's alright to change course and set a new objective or delete it, but ask yourself "Why?" Maybe you need to make it easier for yourself and build your dream in smaller steps.

Although I love technology and I use it to help me, I also use visual aids and I have an annual wall planner that sits above my desk and helps me track my progress. It can look a bit intimidating at the beginning of a busy year – where is the freedom? – but it really helps me see where I am going and identify roadblocks. There are periods where I cannot possibly do everything I'd like to do, and that means I need to re-think or restructure things.

As you do your planning, bear in mind that different objectives will require different approaches. You might need a bit more time to figure this out. It might be worth taking a break at this point to let your subconscious tackle the issue. Put a time in your diary to come back and give it some conscious attention later. Remember, the key activities are to break the plan down into buckets and figure out the processes that need improvement.

Changing Habits

Successfully reaching your goals often means changing your habits. For example, diet and exercise objectives often need a change in lifestyle. That means changing long-term habits and behaviours, which is not easy. You might want to think about getting involved with support groups, both to help you cope and to entrench new values.

Putting things into buckets can help in lots of ways. You can choose your priorities and you can tackle easier tasks first or when your energy levels are low, while maintaining movement towards your objectives and clocking up those motivating "small wins".

For sporting challenges break down every possible aspect of the process and put these into buckets. Looking at the buckets ask yourself – how can I make these easier or better?

Buckets might include things like diet, training hours, technique, researching new methods and approaches, finding a better coach, re-contracting with the coach you have, cross-training to make your workouts more effective, or reading books about sporting achievement, like *The Chimp Paradox* by Dr Steven Peters or *How Champions Think* by Dr Bob Rotella. Remember that small changes in multiple areas can add up to impressive performance improvements overall.

A big project might mean you invest in some apps and project tools to help you put in the hours needed to achieve your dream.

Figure out what you can do to support your objectives. There's so much information out there, particularly on the internet; it's fun to find out more about what increases your effectiveness. I've written more about changing habits in Chapter 12 – Change and choice.

Conclusion

At this point you will either have a plan in place, or at least the makings of one, that will set you on the road to great. The hardest part is to deliver on the plan, but you know that already, don't you?

That is where integrity comes in.

If I was your coach we would have an initial deep conversation to discuss your values. Who are you really? What are your deepest dreams and fears? What do you really want to get out of your life? For many clients, this one session is the most important conversation they ever have.

We all had dreams when we were young, but very few people achieve those dreams. Some don't have the talent, others don't have the grit. We touched on grit only briefly in this book, but it's the thing that keeps you going, even when you feel sick, tired and miserable. Even through tragedy.

Not everyone has the talent and grit to achieve their dreams, and not everyone is prepared to put in the work that it takes either. That's why it's important to explore what you really want and to set themes that resonate with who *you* are.

You may be ambitious at work, but value even more the time spent at home with your family. You might decide you want to explore new things; maybe you want to have the simple pleasures of cooking, reading, travelling or gardening, while keeping a stable job that allows you to fund that life. You may want your job to be in an enjoyable environment where you can be happy and fulfilled and also have time to do the things you really want and enjoy.

For others, the opposite might be true. You might be a relentless overachiever who needs growth and promotion to feel rewarded and you're prepared to put the effort in. Or maybe you're an introvert and you need to put some effort into your interpersonal skills, which become increasingly important as you become more senior. Many introverts make brilliant leaders, by the way. It's not an impediment at all, you just need to work on the skills.

Use this book to help you invest the time in understanding what you want out of your life, and more immediately, out of this year. Be proactive about your life's direction. Take charge of your world.

Believe that further shore may be reachable from here.

Appendix I

Sources of information and learning.

Before going to the bookstore, I heartily recommend TED Talks. Start with the most popular, like Simon Sinek's *Start With Why*. Search for TED Talks on Leadership and choose topics that interest you.

The next source of high-quality, free information is the *Harvard Business Review*. They generously give you access to three articles a month, and again, you can search for topics like leadership, HR, operations management or strategy. Even if all you do is read those three free articles per month, you'll know far more than most of your colleagues after just one year.

Senior leaders also need a view of the world. For that my favourite recommendation is *The Economist*. Although it's expensive and rather dry in tone, reading even one copy a month will give you a good grasp of global issues and trends. I'm lucky, my brother gives it to me as a Christmas present every year and I make sure to read some of every issue and lots from many issues. It's no exaggeration to say that if you read *The Economist*, you can join the conversation at any table in the world.

Books

Between work and relaxation, I read dozens of books a year. I can devour a major book in a day, though I prefer to savour them for longer. When I read lists of the '100 Best Business books' or '100 Best Books on Leadership', I generally find I've read 30%–50%, sometimes more, of any list. Of all these books, there are only a few that make my all-time greats list. These are the ones that I give to friends and clients as presents and that I return to again and again. At the moment, these are my top stars.

Thinking, Fast and Slow by Daniel Kahneman

I love this book so much that I based my MPhil thesis on the underlying theory presented by Daniel Kahneman. His main argument is that although the field of economics is based on the premise that humans are rational decision makers, in real life we make irrational decisions and often poor choices. He goes on to explore why we do this. Highly accessible and brilliantly written, this is the 21st century book for anyone who wants to understand how the mind works.

Man's Search for Meaning by Victor Frankl

A short book that tells Victor Frankl's experience of being in the Nazi concentration camps. The concept "it's not what happens to you, it's how you handle it that counts" comes from Frankl and in this book he talks about the utterly appalling treatment he and the other prisoners endured at the camps and how he survived. The story is terrible, but the message is one of hope.

Frankl said, "Everything can be taken from a man but one thing; the last of the human freedoms – to choose one's attitude in any given set of circumstances, to choose one's ways". He also reminds us that "between stimulus and response there is a space. In that space is our power to choose our response. In our response lies our growth and freedom".

This is one of the most beautiful and powerful books I have ever read. No matter how tough life can be, no matter how badly others treat us and how little control we have, we can still choose our response.

The Chimp Paradox by Dr Steven Peters

I've given away more copies of this book than any other. I also credit it for developing my mind – as Colette De Vries helped me develop my body in order to achieve my own childhood dream: riding internationally under my country's flag. Steven Peters worked with Team UK cyclists ahead of the London Olympics and they dominated the medal board with best-ever results. He has taken his winning philosophy and put it into a book that can help everyone, whether in business or in sport. What I love about the book is that it's based on solid academic research but is written for the ordinary reader. If you want to achieve better results in your working life, your sporting life or both, read this one.

Legacy by James Kerr

This was the first audiobook I listened to and I realised they are a great way to increase my reading capacity. *Legacy* is the story of how the All Blacks rugby team achieved their phenomenal success from the mid-2000s onwards. They took a huge body of knowledge about leadership and sporting excellence and applied it in detail. There's so much here – about humility, about lifelong learning, about putting your very best self on the field, and much more. I draw from it as a leader and a sportswoman and share many of Kerr's points in this book. In fact, my concept of dividing your life or business into different buckets and then making progress in each area came from an idea in *Legacy*, where the team identified all areas of the game and then aimed to make a minimum 1% improvement in each. I do that in my own sport now, at quite a fine level of detail, and when I get it right it makes the difference between winning and losing. *Legacy* is written in a straightforward, highly enjoyable style. Of course it will resonate best if you know and love the game of rugby.

Emotional Intelligence

Social Intelligence

Focus

All by Daniel Goleman

Daniel Goleman is a seminal author when it comes to leadership. Of all his works, I particularly enjoy these three. Goleman is an academic and an original thinker, yet his style is readable and accessible.

Tools of Titans by Tim Ferriss

I have a love-hate relationship with Tim Ferriss because he makes me feel completely inadequate. He is a one man walking experiment, ahead of the trend on everything, but his works really are useful. Just two examples. The first is the use of virtual assistants, which he promoted in *The 4-Hour Work Week*. It took me a while to figure out how to use them, but once I did, I never looked back. You'll find my own current favourite, Hey Jude, in the section on apps.

The second comes from *Tools of Titans*, a compendium of useful information from a range of great thinkers. I've been struggling to sleep for the last few years and have not wanted to resort to sleeping pills. Ferriss recommends two tablespoons of apple cider vinegar and a tablespoon of honey, topped up with hot water in a mug and sipped as tea before bedtime. Bizarre sounding, but it works. I'm sleeping again. If I do wake up during the night I manage to get back to sleep, whereas before I would lie awake worrying for hours.

His books are stuffed with ideas – there's probably something for everyone – and *Tools of Titans* is well worth having on your bookshelf as a reference.

Chase the Rainbow by Poorna Bell

In my life I have had to deal with mental health issues of my own, caused mostly by death and profound loss which is hard, but also a natural consequence of grief and the grieving process. I have shared this road with others, some very close to me. This book by Poorna Bell is one that resonates deeply with me and it is one of the most beautiful and sympathetic descriptions I have ever read of what it is like to love, live with and lose a person with mental health problems. Although I believe in the power of choice, love is not always a choice.

Appendix II

Summary of the 5-Step process

Step 1 – Review the past year

Take a notepad and write down what you've achieved in the year. Think about things like:

- ambitions that you achieved;

- creative work;

- new skills you've developed or new behaviours you've learned;

- work successes;

- your network – people you met or got to know better;

- places you visited;

- things you achieved at home;

- your health; and

- family highlights.

Now write down any disappointments. Things like:

- setbacks at work;

- health issues;

- moments where you had to change plans or face difficulties;

- blocks or hurdles to achieving what you want;

- financial or practical challenges; and

- difficult family or friend situations.

If you did this exercise last year, now is the time to look back at that. Compare what you aimed to achieve with your actual achievements.

Next, write a headline for the last 12 months.

If you were being interviewed and asked to describe the year, what would you say? Don't be too hard on yourself – sometimes it's the journey that's important, not the goal.

Step 2 – Set your themes for this year

Steps 2 and 3 are the really fun part of this entire process and deliver the most important outcome in terms of helping you to understand where you should focus your efforts. Even if you don't see yourself as a creative person, you'll find this part invigorating, not just because it's creative, but because it's about you. First you'll set themes. These are the areas of your life that you feel need attention and change.

We're not looking at specifics here – use your reflections on the past year to help you set your themes for this year.

Write down your top three themes.

Not more than three. If you achieve them early you can add more, but for now focus on these.

Here are some suggestions to kick start your thinking process: work; business; money; leadership; skills development; work/life balance; time-management; productivity; fitness and health; family and friends; fun; travel and exploration; home; love and relationships; giving back.

Step 3 – Identify your priorities

Now you're going to brainstorm by inducing a state of "flow". This helps your creative process by reaching a deeper state of thinking about your themes. It might sound unlikely, but, concentrating really hard on one thing for five minutes helps you make interesting new connections. Don't be disappointed if it doesn't though – it might be that you need to spend more time on this later, as your plan evolves.

Take a piece of paper and a pen. Write down your first theme and, for at least five minutes (set the timer on your phone), write down ideas about how your life could be better a year from today. Concentrate on outcomes; the best possible outcomes you can imagine. This is the time to dream.

Keep the pen moving, draw as well as write, get it all down. Don't lift the pen from the page for the whole five minutes. As you do this exercise remember to be ambitious; put no limits on what you could achieve.

Build on your ideas. If you want to be creative, what does it look like? A book, a painting course, finding a way to take your team to a new level of delivery?

Keep less glamorous objectives in mind; maybe you need to address some aspect of your health or well-being?

Try to be specific – it's not "get fit", it's run 15km a week or walk the Otter Trail. Think about outcomes; the best outcomes you can imagine. Thinking about outcomes is the clever thing about this exercise because it helps crystallise what you really want and to put it into words. Be bold and brave at this point. Later you can refine. For now, dream of the best possible outcomes.

Now do the same for the next two themes.

You should find this process exciting and invigorating, and as you get into it, you may find that one of your priorities starts to take precedence. That is good news because it means the exercise is helping you to prioritise better.

Ideas might emerge that surprise you. This exercise can be a way of tapping into your subconscious; of pulling out ambitions and thinking that may have been lost over the last year as more urgent thoughts take over. Don't reject any surprising thoughts; they may be the important ones.

Some people have dreams that appear huge and aspirational: write a book; earn a million Rands; raise a million Dollars; start a PhD. Other people's dreams might be more practical or personal: lose weight; get fit; learn to cook really well; take your dream vacation. Does it matter? Of course not. These are *your* dreams: this is what you need to be focus on now, given the current circumstances of your life.

When you've done all three, take a short break.

Step 4 – Set your goals for the year

After the break, return to your "dream sheets" and circle the ideas and objectives that appeal to you the most or seem the most important, or both. You want to feel inspired and excited and you want these things to have a positive impact on your life.

Now write them down as a list.

Aim for about three objectives per theme – a maximum of nine. If it's a big one – like earning an important new qualification – you can focus on just that. You should end up with three to nine objectives.

Now start to break those objectives down into tasks, or create a schedule that will start you on the road to achieving them. Some of your objectives will mean changing your habits, so make sure you don't try to achieve too much at once.

Now, let's turn those plans into actions...

Step 5 – Turn your plans into actions

Take a calendar and mark up the commitments already in place.

Choose one objective from your list and write down what you must do in January, February and March to be on track to achieve it by the end of March.

If it's going to take longer, spread your actions throughout the year, but make detailed plans of your steps for the first quarter.

Write down your objectives, print them out and keep them on your desk.

Keep a date with yourself at the start of every month to check on your progress.

References

Amabile, T.M., & Kramer, S.J. 2011. The power of small wins. *Harvard Business Review, 89*(5), pp. 70-80.

Arnot, S. 2018. *That Further Shore: Turn Your Dreams into Goals and Make Them Reality*. Bryanston: KR Publishing.

Branson, R. 2011. *Losing my virginity how I survived, had fun, and made a fortune doing business my way*. New York: Crown Business.

Cardone, G. 2011. *The 10X rule: The only difference between success and failure*. Hoboken, NJ: John Wiley & Sons.

Clear, J. 2018. *About James Clear*. Retrieved from: http://www.jamesclear.com

Colvin, G. 2008. *Talent is overrated: what really separates world-class performers from everybody else*. London: Penguin.

Covey, S.R. 2013. *The 7 habits of highly effective people: Powerful lessons in personal change*. New York: Simon and Schuster.

Csikszentmihalyi, M. 1997. *Finding flow: The psychology of engagement with everyday life*. New York: Basic Books.

Dalio, R. 2017. *Principles: life and work*. New York: Simon and Schuster.

Emerson, D. 2011. *How good riders get good: Daily choices that lead to success in any equestrian sport*. North Pomfret, VT: Trafalgar Square Books.

Frankl, V. E. 1985. *Man's search for meaning*. New York: Simon and Schuster.

Ferriss, T., Schwarzenegger, A., & Geoffroi, R. 2017. *Tools of titans: The tactics, routines, and habits of billionaires, icons, and world-class performers*. Boston: Houghton Mifflin Harcourt.

Gladwell, M. 2008. *Outliers: The story of success*. London: Hachette UK.

Goleman, D. 2006. *Emotional intelligence*. New York: Bantam.

Goleman, D. 2007. *Social intelligence: The new science of human relationships*. London: Arrow.

Goleman, D. 2013. *Focus*. New York: Harper Audio.

Goleman, D. 2015. *Focus: The hidden driver of excellence*. New York: Harper.

Harrison, K. 2018. *The 5:2 Diet and me!* Retrieved from: http://kate- harrison.com/5-2diet.

Ho, S.-Y., Tong, E.M.W., & Jia, L. 2016. Authentic and hubristic pride: Differential effects on delay of gratification. *Emotion, 16*(8), pp. 1147-1156.

Kahneman, D. 2015. *Thinking, fast and slow*. New York: Farrar, Straus and Giroux.

Kerr, J. 2013. *Legacy: 15 lessons in leadership: What the All Blacks can teach us about the business of life*. London: Constable.

Kolb, D.A. 2015. *Experiential learning: Experience as the source of learning and development*. Upper Saddle River, NY: Pearson Education.

Lucas, B.J., & Nordgren, L.F. 2015. People underestimate the value of persistence for creative performance. *Journal of personality and social psychology, 109*(2), p. 232.

Matthews, G. 2011. *Study Backs up Strategies for Achieving Goals*. Retrieved from: http://www.dominican.edu/dominicannews/study-backs-up-strategies-for-achievinggoals.

Peters, S. 2012. *The chimp paradox: The mind management programme to help you achieve success, confidence and happiness*. London: Vermilion.

Rotella, R.J., & Cullen, R. 2015. *How champions think: In sports and in life*. New York: Simon & Schuster.

Schwarzenegger, A. 2013. *Total recall: my unbelievably true life story*. New York: Simon and Schuster.

Syed, M. 2015. *Black box thinking: Why most people never learn from their mistakes-but some do*. New York: Portfolio/Penguin.

Valdesolo, P., & DeSteno, D. 2011. Synchrony and the social tuning of compassion. *Emotion, 11*(2), p. 262.

Vohs, K.D., Baumeister, R.F., Schmeichel, B.J., Twenge, J.M., Nelson, N.M., & Tice, D.M. 2008. Making choices impairs subsequent self-control: A limited-resource account of decision making, self-regulation, and active initiative. *Journal of Personality and Social Psychology, 94*(5), pp. 883-898. DOI: 10.1037/0022-3514.94.5.883.

www.ingramcontent.com/pod-product-compliance
Lightning Source LLC
Chambersburg PA
CBHW060351090426
42734CB00011B/2108